FAITH'S PLACE

IØ11Ø21Ø

"This book is a timely consideration of church-state relations. It offers a number of different perspectives on the interaction between the Western democratic political model—itself under considerable pressure from internal and external forces—and religion in those societies. This is particularly apposite to Australia, a country that has had historically a strongly secular culture but where active hostility to religious views has sharply increased in recent years amongst so-called progressive elements in the community."

MICHAEL SEXTON SC

author of

Dissenting Opinions

"Concerns about the viability of democracy, the decline of institutional religion, and the resurgence of individualism are expressed with increasing frequency in Western societies. Awareness of these developments has been heightened by the impact of the global coronavirus pandemic. In this important book, Bryan Turner and Damien Freeman, together with the scholars who have contributed responses to their essays, examine the implications of significant societal changes for the vitality of civil society and assess the role that religion might continue to play in the lives of individuals and communities."

PETER KURTI

author of

Sacred and Profane:
Faith and Belief in a Secular Society

"Faith's Place breaks new ground on essential questions: how can secularising societies cope with the persistence of religious belief—and how does the failure to do so jeopardise democracy itself? Timely, absorbing, and erudite, this meditation is a must-read for anyone concerned with the fate of self-government not only in Australia, but across the societies of the Western world."

MARY EBERSTADT

author of

How the West Really Lost God:
A New Theory of Secularization

THE KAPUNDA PRESS

an imprint of Connor Court Publishing
in association with the PM Glynn Institute

GENERAL EDITOR
Damien Freeman
PM Glynn Institute
Australian Catholic University

CHALICE OF LIBERTY
PROTECTING RELIGIOUS FREEDOM IN AUSTRALIA
Frank Brennan – M. A. Casey – Greg Craven

TODAY'S TYRANTS
RESPONDING TO DYSON HEYDON
J. D. Heydon – Frank Brennan – Anne Henderson – Paul Kelly
M. A. Casey – Peter Kurti – M. J. Crennan – Hayden Ramsay
Shireen Morris – Michael Ondaatje – Sandra Lynch
Catherine Renshaw

FEDERATION'S MAN OF LETTERS
PATRICK MCMAHON GLYNN
Anne Henderson – Anne Twomey – Suzanne Rutland
Patrick Mullins – John Fahey – Peter Boyce

NONSENSE ON STILTS
RESCUING HUMAN RIGHTS IN AUSTRALIA
M. A. Casey – Damien Freeman – Catherine Renshaw
Nicholas Aroney – Emma Dawson – Terri Butler – Jennifer Cook
Bryan Turner – Tim Wilson

The Market's Morals

RESPONDING TO JESSE NORMAN

Jesse Norman – Marc Stears – Greg Melleuish – Adrian Pabst
Amanda Walsh – Parnell McGuinness – Michael Easson
David Corbett – Tom Switzer – Cris Abbu – Tanya Aspland
Leanne Smith – M. A. Casey

Story of Our Country

LABOR'S VISION FOR AUSTRALIA
Adrian Pabst

Tribalism's Troubles

RESPONDING TO ROWAN WILLIAMS

Rowan Williams – Ethan Westwood – M. A. Casey
Cristina Gomez – Nigel Zimmermann – Annette Pierdziwol
Kerry Pinkstone – Amanda Stoker – Scott Stephens
Ben Etherington – Anthony Ekpo – Austin Wyatt – Sandra Jones

The New Social Contract

RENEWING THE LIBERAL VISION FOR AUSTRALIA
Tim Wilson

Forthcoming:
Hope in Common

REGAINING CONFIDENCE IN DEMOCRACY

Scott Stephens – Adrian Pabst – Damien Freeman – Julian Leeser
Alda Balthrop-Lewis – Richard Colledge – Karen Jones
Suzanne Killmister – Luke Bretherton – M. A. Casey

— FAITH'S —
PLACE

— *Democracy* —
in a Religious World

BRYAN S. TURNER & DAMIEN T. FREEMAN

THE KAPUNDA PRESS

Copyright © 2020 as a collection, Damien Freeman; individual chapters, the contributors.

ALL RIGHTS RESERVED. This book contains material protected under International and Federal Copyright Laws and Treaties. Any unauthorised reprint or use of this material is prohibited. No part of this book may be reproduced or transmitted in any form or by any means, electronic or mechanical, including photocopying, recording, or by any information storage and retrieval system without express written permission from the publisher.

CONNOR COURT PUBLISHING PTY LTD
PO Box 7257
Redland Bay QLD 4165
sales@connorcourt.com www.connorcourt.com

Cover picture: Elric Ringstad, *Untitled 4* (c.2019), oil, bees wax, damar on canvas.

ISBN: 9781922449337 (pbk.)

Cover design by Ian James

Printed in Australia

"secularists are wrong when they ask believers to leave their religion at the door before entering into the public square"

Barack Obama
Call to Renewal Keynote Address, 28 June 2006

Contents

Foreword

Mark Coleridge

A S A THEME IN HUMAN HISTORY, the relationship between politics and religion is well worn. However, a new chapter is being written at this time. In the Western world, the hard-won separation of church and state is in some ways being reinterpreted, as we see in the electoral debates in the United States and political manoeuvrings elsewhere. The subtitle of a book I read recently claimed that "being in charge is not what it used to be"; and that is true for both political and religious leaders.

Politics and religion are interacting in new ways at a time when, it was thought, religion had been consigned to a strictly private world. Yet in various guises—not all of them edifying—religious faith keeps claiming a place in the public square, even when dreams of 'throne and altar' are long gone; and some political leaders have seen the advantage of recruiting religion to their cause. Against that background, the question seems to be: How do we accept the separation of church and state—for the good of both—and yet allow the voice of religious faith to be heard in the political process? How do we ensure that proper separation does not mean radical alienation?

The presumption here is that faith speaks not just of God and the things of heaven but also of human beings and the things of earth. This is fundamentally true of biblical religion which has been seminal in shaping the political culture of much of the world we know. What biblical religion can offer the political process is a transcendent vision of the human person which generates a vision of what makes for the flourishing of a truly human society. It was this vision which made the voice of Pope John Paul II so politically compelling and why, in the current maelstrom, Pope Francis can speak in different accents but with authority. The vision itself is not political in any partisan or ideological sense; but it has immense implications for political decision-making. For, without such a framework, the political process runs the risk of becoming no more than a crude power-play in which tactics trump policy at every turn.

Covid-19 may be changing the world in some ways, but it has certainly accelerated processes already in evidence, albeit sluggishly, before the pandemic struck. That is why the appearance of *Faith's Place: democracy in a religious world* is well-timed. It is also good that a wide range of voices is heard in these pages. Dictatorship fears a variety of voices, but democracy depends upon it. For it is only the play of perspectives, even of ideologies, which allows freedom to emerge, so that the symphony we call the common good—rather than any one voice—is decisive in the political process.

Democracy is not what it was; nor is religion. For both to thrive in a way the common good demands, each needs to recognise how the other has changed, which will mean listening respectfully to each other and resisting the absolutist claims born of the world of 'all or nothing'. That will then allow both to enter into the new kind of dialogue which this book imagines and may even make possible.

✠ Mark Coleridge
Archbishop of Brisbane
President, Australian Catholic Bishops Conference
1 September 2020

Introduction:
Waves of democracy and
religion in global history

Damien T. Freeman and Bryan S. Turner

I N THE SPRING OF 1991, the former White House advisor and Harvard political theorist, Samuel P. Huntington, published "Democracy's Third Wave", which rapidly became the classic account and defence of the global success of democracy. The process of democratisation—conceived as a series of waves—was seen to characterize the emergence of democratic governments across the globe from Romania to Nepal.[1] The explanation of this dramatic development included the legitimacy problems of authoritarian states, unprecedented economic growth starting in the 1960s, and a 'snowballing effect' in which one successful transition encouraged other states to follow.

Given the topic our of book, we should, perhaps, begin with Huntington's observation about the significance of change within the Catholic Church for the process of democratisation throughout the world—"A striking shift in the doctrine and activities of the Catholic Church, manifested in the Second Vatican Council of 1963-65 and the transformation of national Catholic churches from defenders of the status quo to opponents of authoritarianism."[2]

Huntington's thesis encouraged researchers to think globally of 'waves of religion' following the collapse of the Soviet Empire, which created opportunities for the re-establishment of the Christian presence across Eastern Europe and beyond. Churches subsequently enjoyed vibrant growth in Africa and many parts of Asia. Democratisation, combining with de-secularisation as liberalisation, in the 1980s appeared to favour religious growth in Sub-Saharan Africa, in the imploding Soviet satellites, and in much of East Asia.

Huntington was not, however, optimistic about the forward momentum of the third wave. In the 1990s, he noted a series of reverse waves as some states reverted to authoritarianism, economic setbacks undercut efforts to promote egalitarianism, and elites resisted the spread of democratic values. He was skeptical that the United States would continue to act as a beacon of democratic ideas and practices. He noted that "American will to promote democracy may or may not be sustained. American ability to do so, on the other hand, is limited."[3]

Professor Huntington died in 2008. How might he have evaluated our current situation, in which both democracy and religion appear to be under threat? Western democracies have suffered a number of setbacks—the 2008-11 financial crisis and subsequent austerity packages; widespread populist politics against the existing political structures; the growth of political extremism; the return of political authoritarianism; and the withdrawal from international collaboration over climate change, free movement of goods and people, and attacks on multiculturalism and cosmopolitanism. In short, there is a crisis of both democracy as a political system and liberalism as a set of values. Is there a crisis of religion?

How has religion fared in this volatile environment from 1991 until 2020? In many of the essays appearing in this volume, the current position of religion is complex to say the least. On the one hand, there is ample evidence of decline—shrinking numbers of people who identify as religious in a conventional sense, declining recruitment to the priesthood and ministry, and in many areas of traditional belief—marriage, sexuality, abortion—the churches appear to be in retreat. On the other hand, there is widespread evidence of spirituality and online or digital religion. In addition, the churches are involved in major debates about the direction of secular society. Hospital chaplains are at the forefront of care for the victims of Covid-19. Churches continue to play a major role in the provision of welfare and shelter to the many who are homeless and fall outside the official welfare system.

Faith's Place was conceived and developed before Australia and other Western democracies were fully in the grip of the Covid-19 pandemic. As we send this manuscript to the publishers in October 2020, it is not clear when the pandemic will be under control; when an effective vaccine will be generally available; or what the long-term consequences might be. Some long-term consequences are, however, already apparent. The first is that the transformative period of modern globalisation, starting around the 1970s, is already over, as the negative effects on health and jobs becomes more evident. The second is that Covid-19 will never be fully eradicated any more than influenza or measles has been eradicated. Indeed, an outbreak of the bubonic plague—the original Black Death—in outer Mongolia was announced by the World Health Organization earlier this year.

While the long-term consequences might be matters of speculation, there are some immediate lessons from the pandemic that relate to our discussion of democracy and religion. The first is that the democracies appear to have had more problems controlling infections than authoritarian states—even allowing for under-reporting. America has faced a significant challenge where individualism, the federal structure, civil unrest, political extremism, and conspiracy theories have made it difficult to impose social distancing, the wearing of masks, and lockdowns. These factors have made it difficult to implement policies that are scientifically credible. The contrast with authoritarian regimes, such as China, Vietnam, and South Korea is striking.

But what of religion? We suggest that traditional religious institutions may go the same way as post-Covid patterns of employment. Responses to the pandemic have shown that many professional people and office workers in general are capable of working at home by the use of modern technology. When Boris Johnson said he wanted to see members of Her Majesty's Home Civil Service back in their offices, senior civil servants said he was out of date. Civil servants were perfectly able to conduct most of their work from home. Working at home reduces the cost of employment to corporations and hence it might be attractive in terms of economic efficiency. The outcome would transform the modern city, such as Sydney, where the rush to build more office space is like shutting the gate after the horses have already bolted. The consequence is to reinforce individualism because the workplace is also a source of community. Perhaps the same consequence might take place in religious institutions, where online services have been developed in response to the threat of infections.

One reasonable conclusion from this brief commentary is that, while churches and their congregations are often criticised for their conservatism in clinging to what are seen to be outdated or harmful values, religion and democracy appear to go hand in hand. As democracy opens up spaces for personal freedom, religion may also thrive. Equally, religious values of respect, charity, and care remain fundamental to urban civility, on which democracy ultimately rests.

This volume has its genesis in one of the workstreams of the PM

Glynn Institute—Australian Catholic University's public policy think-tank—which investigates issues relating to democracy in a religious world. The starting point for this work is the observation that population projections published in the Pew Research Center's 2015 report, *The Future of World Religions: Population Growth Projections 2010-2050*, underscore the fact that the world is becoming more religious, not less, as globalisation and rising living standards outside the developed world continue to bring about far-reaching social and political change. For Australia, as an increasingly diverse but also increasingly secular country, it is important to deepen our understanding of what this reality entails. Countries such as Australia are projected to become more secular, however, the religiously unaffiliated as a share of global population will decline over the next forty years. For Australia, as an increasingly secular country that faces out into a world which is becoming more religious, the challenge will be to ensure that we do not misread a changing situation. Public policy thinking needs to continue to broaden its focus to take religion into account as an enduring part of the social and political landscape and a powerful influence in shaping people's values and behaviour. Turning attention to the role that religion plays more generally in human existence also helps us to respond more effectively when problems arise in areas such as social cohesion and security.

The Institute's object when investigating these issues is not to claim that religion is superior to other social factors that can provide social cohesion, or to argue that faith is the solution to every problem in secular societies, or for that matter to deny that it might contribute to the problems. It is, however, to address the need for a better understanding of the positive contributions that faith communities make to the common good, which tend to be taken for granted and overlooked. It is important that these contributions be understood properly by public policymakers, both as resources for building and renewing a good society, and as something that good public policy should seek to sustain, or at least not inadvertently weaken.

The challenges presented for democracy in a religious world are the subject of this volume. They are addressed from the perspective of the challenges for liberal societies in an essay by Bryan Turner, and from the perspective of the challenges for democratic leaders in an essay by Damien Freeman. There follow eight responses to these essays. First, there are the responses from the perspective of public life: from Dean Smith and Luke Gosling who currently serve in the Australian Parliament, and from Ursula Stephens, who previously served in it. We then turn to the perspectives from the academy: from Jocelyne Cesari, Robert Hefner, and David Saperstein, who write from beyond these shores; and Riaz Hassan and James Franklin, who write from within Australia. Finally, the Institute's director, Michael Casey, offers some conclusions about these responses from the perspective of Catholic intellectual life.

Bryan Turner addresses the question of the relationship between religion and democracy in Australia through the prism of society. He reflects on what it would mean for people living in Australia to be happy, and to what extent Australian society's capacity to deliver this is helped or hindered by its society's commitment to democracy and/or its commitment to religion. He approaches Australian society as a fundamentally liberal society, and identifies eight themes to be addressed in order to draw conclusions about religion and democracy in Australia: multiculturalism and the place it makes for religious groups; the experience of Aboriginal communities; the status of citizenship and the country's record in terms of human rights; the rise of modern individualism and the loss of community that accompanies it; the decline of rural churches and townships; the erosion of civility and its consequences for democracy; the extreme politics that has emerged on both the left and right; and the perennial quest for balancing church and state. His conclusions are challenging: there is no strong message about the success of democracy in Australia, and there are many big questions about the future of religion in Australia which remain unanswered.

Damien Freeman addresses the question of the relationship between religion and democracy in Australia through the prism of leadership. He observes that as Australia becomes less religious, it is likely that political leaders will have less affinity with religion and, indeed, that it might become incomprehensible to them. He reflects on J. D. Heydon QC's observations about the extent to which the 'modern elites' already demonstrate antipathy towards religion in Australia, and suggests that one factor contributing to this state of affairs might be incomprehension of religion. He draws on Michael Sandel's conception of the 'encumbered self' as a way into understanding what might otherwise seem incomprehensible about the individual's duty to adhere to religious conscience, and Rabbi Jonathan Sacks's 'dignity of difference' as a way into understanding what might otherwise seem incomprehensible about the need to respect the ethical consequences of belonging to a religious community. In this way, he offers suggestions for how future leaders in an increasingly non-religious Australia might overcome their incomprehension of the religious commitments of communities within Australia and in an increasingly religious world.

In response to these essays, Dean Smith, Luke Gosling, and Ursula Stephens write from the perspective of those within Australian public life. Gosling offers some reflections on the way in which parliamentarians' personal religious faith can inform their approach to democratic leadership. Smith suggests that two features of Australian democracy offer a procedural solution to the problems identified by Turner and Freeman. Stephens chooses to focus more on the fellowship dimension: how religious fellowship is able to bridge political divides within the Parliament, and how the current pandemic invites us to take more seriously the importance of fellowship in society at large.

Robert Hefner, Jocelyne Cesari, and David Saperstein offer a quite different perspective, writing, as they do, both from outside of public life and from outside of Australia. Hefner agrees with much of the analyses offered by Turner and Freeman, but he seeks to widen the picture they paint, warning that the situation is even more complicated than they suggest. Yes, individualism is corroding the sense of solidarity necessary for both citizenship and religion, but there are other processes at work that are giving rise to new forms of association and self-identification, and it is important that we appreciate these, if we are to address their most serious effects—increasing polarisation and decreasing civility that threaten liberal democracy. Cesari broadens out Turner and Freeman's analyses in a different direction. She agrees with their approach to the reciprocal influence of religion and democracy on one another. She suggests that the real challenge, however, lies not in understanding that religion is important for democracy, but in gaining clarity about the sense in which it informs democracy: namely, that religion is as much about behaviour and belonging as it is about belief, and this means the political dimension of religion cannot meaningfully be extracted from the public square or the secular space. Whilst Saperstein salutes Turner and Freeman's shared commitment to religious freedom, he finds himself at odds with their conclusions about its future. He draws on his own experience to compare Turner's analysis of Australian society with his sometimes differing experience of American society, and challenges Freeman's use of Sandel's 'encumbered selves' and Sacks's 'dignity of difference', all of which enables him to arrive at different conclusions about the enduring relevance of international human rights for the protection of religious freedom.

Riaz Hassan and James Franklin then focus in on two specific issues raised by Turner and Freeman. Hassan takes up Turner's discussion about the challenge of multiculturalism and in particular of Muslims in Australia, offering a more in-depth analysis of the problem of Islamophobia. Franklin takes up Freeman's discussion of the difficulties that non-religious leaders face in taking religion seriously, and offers a deeper analysis of the problem of incomprehension of religion in Australia.

The volume concludes with an essay by Michael Casey, in which he reflects on the observations other contributors have made. He suggests that these reflections help us to identify blind spots that the secular world has when confronted by religion's persisting influence.

In their own way, each of the essays in this collection invites us to focus our attention on the future of democracy and religion. Looking to the past, democracy may not owe much to religion generally, or Christianity in particular, but secularism and liberalism most definitely do. We live in a world that often characterizes religion, not least Christianity, as the enemy of secular and liberal society. So it is well to remember that it was Christian ideas that were as central to the emergence of the division between church and state that forms the basis of modern secularism, as Greek ideas were to the birth of democracy; and that it was Christian ideas about the dignity of each human being that gave rise to the liberal social order that is a hallmark of modern Western societies.

And yet, the liberal and secular world that grew out of Christendom sometimes seems to struggle to accommodate any religion, let alone Christianity, in a meaningful way. Thus, it is timely to reflect on the challenges that liberal and secular democracies currently present for religion, and those that the persisting influence of religion present for democracy. Is religion an asset or a liability for a democracy? If it is necessary or desirable to accommodate religion within democracy, what are the challenges presented for doing so in twenty-first-century Australia, in Western societies more generally, and, indeed, in the world at large?

The cover of this volume contains a detail from an untitled painting by the contemporary Australian artist, Elric Ringstad. The canvas has a monochrome background that evokes Philip Larkin's image of "the deep blue air, that shows Nothing, and is nowhere, and is endless"—disturbed only by the lonely wanderings of Wordsworth's cloud "that floats on high o'er vales and hills". In place of the vales and hills, however, are three black crosses joined together by a simple black arabesque flourish. To a certain cast of mind, it is merely a public utility: three telegraph poles supporting a couple of street lights depicted in silhouette. To another cast of mind, however, it might evoke a faint vision of the skyline at Calvary on that first Good Friday. In one way or another, it might express more of the transcendent than it actually depicts, if not the Light of the World, perhaps something of Wordsworth's sublime Lake District or Larkin's High Windows. Just as the artist's rendering of this pedestrian scene puts the spectator in mind loftier things than are immediately apparent in the picture, so too the business of liberal societies and democratic leaders prompt us to return our attention to the waves of religion whose persisting influence—however unexpected that may be—repays ethically serious reflection.

Two approaches to understanding democracy in a religious world

Liberal societies in a religious world

Bryan S. Turner

T HE DEBATE ABOUT the secular character of modern societies has yet to achieve stable conclusion. The original certainty that modernity meant secularisation and secularism has disappeared, but it is unclear what is in its place. There is general agreement that the mainstream churches are in decline, but there is ample evidence of spirituality, religious life outside the churches, the growth of digital religion, religious vitality in Africa, and to some extent in China. Perhaps the most relevant issues for reflecting on religion and democracy are, firstly, the nature of 'public religions' such as Catholicism and Solidarity in Poland, the American religious right, liberation theology in Latin America, or the Shia Revolution.[1] Secondly, to what extent have manifestations of civil religions, perhaps most notably in the United States, become important developments in otherwise secular society?[2] We might agree that modern societies are secular, but that obituaries for religion are premature.

But what about democracy? Although answers to the question, "what is religion?" are unclear, there is much less dispute about what defines democracy. The number of ingredients is, however, lengthy: universal suffrage, free elections, legitimacy of opposition, the rule of law, independence of the judiciary, separation of church and state, and more. There is equally open agreement that Western democracies are in trouble as most of the 'ingredients' are under attack. The crisis of Western democracies is deep but relatively recent, namely associated with the financial crisis and its consequences in the first decade of this century, the impact of populism and extreme politics (on the left and right), terrorism, the erosion of the role of law, the failures of leadership and parliamentary democracy, the corruption of the elite, the alienation of the citizenry, and growing forms of racism.[3] As I write this essay in March 2020, Covid-19 threatens to undermine Western democracies and to change the shape of the world's population. In response to Donald Trump, will we be in our churches this coming Easter, or in our graves? Covid-19 may strengthen religion as people search for hope and consolation but it could also be the dark side of religion; the apocalypse.

Bringing these two debates together, is religion part of the problem or part of the solution of democracy? As an opening statement, there is a well-established view in political theory and political history that Protestantism played an important part in laying the foundations of democracy by translating the Bible into the vernacular, raising the status of the laity through independent chapels, rejecting the idea of the keys of grace, and limiting the sacerdotal claims of priesthood. Special attention is often given, for example, to Methodism in promoting the role and authority of the laity and of lay leadership. A modern-day version of Methodism is Pentecostalism.

In this academic debate, Roman Catholicism was given a correspondingly critical interpretation of its negative relationship to democracy. In the twentieth century, its opposition to secular Communism often placed it in support of right-wing, indeed fascist, political parties and governments. The support of the church for 'bureaucratic authoritarianism' in Latin America is a prime example. However, this standard interpretation neglects the role of Basista Catholicism in bringing an end to authoritarian military regimes in the twentieth century.[4] In addition, the relationship of Catholicism to democracy and modernity changed after Vatican II. We also have to take into account the role of the Catholic Church in promoting Christian democracy within the European Union.[5] Catholicism is also said to have played a role in the rise of human rights through the development of 'personalism' and the idea of 'human dignity'—ideas that eventually provided a basis for the Universal Declaration of Human Right.[6]

There is an alternative approach to this issue which does not hinge on differences between different branches of Christianity or indeed on different religions. This alternative approach argues that a vibrant civil religion is an important foundation for democracy. Religious chapels, congregations, or communities are foundational to civil society, which is where ordinary citizens live their lives and go about making families, raising children, and committing themselves to the life of the community. It is within this network of communities, groups, voluntary associations, school boards, and clubs that citizenship and civility are fostered and nurtured. These activities typically take place outside the control or surveillance of the state, and yet these pillars of the community are the ultimate source of good manners and good government, indeed of the good society. These practices are an important brake on the individualism which is the inevitable offspring of liberalism. I take this argument to be the basis of one of the most influential studies of democracy by the French aristocrat, Alexis de Tocqueville, who made an observational tour of colonial America in 1831 and published *Democracy in America* in 1835 and 1840.[7] Whereas in Europe political existence had been created by the upper echelons of society, in America the community existed before the society and the state, and the state before the Union. His account of the communal basis of

American democracy and the limitations of the state apparatus remains a classic account of American liberal democracy.

Turning to recent history, with the fall of the Berlin Wall and the end of the Cold War, the prospects for liberal democracy were bright and optimistic. However, political life is perhaps inevitably never stable, and the optimism of the last century changed quickly. The attack on the Twin Towers in 2011 changed American foreign policy and American self-confidence irrevocably. The financial crisis of 2008-2011 transformed economic policies as states adopted austerity packages to manage their financial problems. We now appear to face a range of daunting crises for democracies—the widespread growth of populism, the rise of political extremism of the left and right, white extremism and violent forms of masculinity, the changing power relations between the United States, China, and Russia, the crisis in the Ukraine, the consequences of climate change, international relations, and the wars in the Middle East under the presidency of Donald Trump, the Brexit crisis and the potential damage of Brexit to the European Union. I have already alluded to the threat of Covid-19, but perhaps I should add that its consequences point in two directions. The pandemic, especially if the outbreak continues through 2020, will pose severe threats to liberal democracies with the limitations on individual freedoms that are necessary to quarantine large cities. These developments may undermine the globalisation of travel, labour markets, consumerism, tourism, and economic production through global corporations. Is this the end of globalisation as we have known it for the last century? The alternative outcome might be more optimistic and underline the cosmopolitanism that has been evolving as a companion to liberal democracies. This second alternative involves increasing co-operation between nations via what legal theorists call 'common necessity'. An early example is the commitment to the freedom of travel across the world's oceans. The Covid-19 pandemic has seen nations co-operate to close borders, share medical supplies, and oppose the spread of fake news. There is no reason to believe that Covid-19 is the last pandemic. There will be more pandemics as a consequence of a globalised world and hence there will be future necessities for international co-operation.

What is the place of religion in these political changes? There are several issues involving religion in the public domain: the place of Muslim minorities in Western democracies, the growth of Islamophobia; the rise of antisemitism including attacks on synagogues; and the definition of European boundaries by reference to Christendom. Is there a general fear of Islam in the West?[8] Has it been intensified by the crisis in the Middle East? While Christian leaders, specifically the Pope, have played a major role in defending the rights of refugees, asylum seekers, and the stateless, Christianity is often invoked by the far right as a defining characteristic of the West to the exclusion of other traditions. The growth of Muslim communities is simply one aspect of the large issues about multiculturalism, civic nationalism, and growing diversity. Criticism of multiculturalism is not new.[9] The growth of populist politics in both Europe and the United States has opened up a political space where open criticism of immigration, multiculturalism, and social diversity has grown and is no longer easily dismissed as prejudiced or racist. Debate, criticism, and opposition are, after all, the hallmarks of liberal democracy. The only proviso is that debate has to be, in Rawlsian terms, 'reasonable' or in terms of this chapter, 'civil'.

In this essay, I want to consider these large and threatening issues in the context of a broader set of debates regarding secularisation and the changing nature of religion in terms of spirituality, religious practice outside the churches, the role of religion in civil society, and the relationship of religion to civility, which I argue is a basic value of democracy as a political system and to liberalism as a set of values. I argue that we are moving into a period of incivility associated with many of the developments I have just identified: political extremism, populism, the erosion of citizenship, and the corruption of elites.

My principal thesis, therefore, is that the forces that are changing and eroding citizenship and democracy are the same forces that are changing and undermining religion. As our world becomes more individualised and our communal life shrinks, so religion is transformed into a placeless spirituality of the individual, who is increasingly understood as a consumer of both secular and religious goods and services.[10] Religious and political life are subject to the same consumer forces of an advanced economy. Thus, "modern religious formations are profoundly influenced by the commodification of everyday life. Religion becomes part of the global economic system in terms of the circulation of religious commodities (amulets, prayer books, pilgrimages and so forth), by the creation and promotion of religious lifestyles (often associated with body management, veiling, diet and dining), by the adoption of modern communication technologies and so on."[11] This conclusion inevitably involves a normative judgment in claiming that just as social solidarity becomes thinner, the same judgement applies to religion. It is perhaps in this context—and only in this context—that the rational choice model of religion actually fits, namely supply-side theories of religion appear to work in a neoliberal era. According to American sociologists Rodney Stark and William Bainbridge, in *A Theory of Religion,* churches are 'firms', selling 'salvation goods' in a competitive market where efficiency is maximised in the absence of monopolies.[12] The demand for religious goods is anthropologically constant; only supply is variable, and hence the rational model is a supply-side theory. The rational choice model of religion rejects the secularisation thesis, arguing instead that once the religious market is freed from state regulation, consumers enjoy greater choice and variety. This interpretation explains why religion has greater vitality in the United States than in Europe.

In this essay, I now proceed to consider eight broad issues that are constitutive of the problems and prospects of both religion and democracy. I start with issues around social diversity and religious difference under the broad heading of multiculturalism with special reference to Australia. The modern history of Australian social diversity starts with the end of white Australia and the building of multiculturalism. The white Australia policy began with the Immigration Act of 1909 and came to a legal conclusion with a number of amendments introduced by the Labor prime minister, Gough Whitlam. Multicultural development has been the key feature of modern Australian society. I dwell on the issue of multiculturalism and the changing composition of Australian society because it is the necessary basis for any discussion of religion, diversity, and democracy. Australian ideas about multiculturalism had their origin in the end of the white Australia policy, but it aimed at the integration of white Europeans. Multicultural policies are often thought to be at a critical turning point in competition with various shades of nationalism—civic and religious.

Generally speaking, while there was initial opposition to social and cultural diversity, Australians have typically thought of Australia as a successful multicultural society. Donald Horne's *The Lucky Country* is typically invoked when commentators want a benchmark of success or subsequent failure of Australia as a modern, secular, parliamentary democracy.[13] Horne (1922-2005) was a successful author, journalist, and editor, whose 1964 publication caused an immediate storm of discussion and debate. *The Lucky Country* is often referenced in connection with Australia's stability as a democracy in addition to a successful economy, despite the financial crisis of 2008-2011.The idea of good luck and success is often attached to Australia becoming a successful multicultural society as Greeks, Eastern Europeans, people from the Commonwealth, and people of different religious traditions made their homes here. Horne's message was in fact critical of

Australia when in his conclusion he said that we were a society of "second rate people", with poor leadership and a dependence in both culture and politics on a British legacy. Our wealth was based on mineral extraction rather than new technologies and innovation. Horne might equally have called his publication *The Unlucky Country* but the popularity of the book and its title have resisted interrogation.

Modern evaluations of Australia's success story continue to be, perhaps inevitably, mixed. We rank 22nd in the world in terms of economic innovation. Although the economy remains strong, much of our economic growth has been driven by the property market, where soaring prices have put home ownership out of reach of the majority of young people. Our record, with regard to Aboriginal rights, is much criticised in the human rights literature. The slow death of the Great Barrier Reef and the devastating bushfires of 2019-2020 have raised serious concerns about the climate and the environment. However, in the introduction to this essay, I am more concerned with the question of the success or otherwise of multiculturalism.

Has multiculturalism been a success or are we a nation of parallel communities? The evidence regarding the integration of Muslim communities is mixed. If success means integration rather than assimilation, then there is evidence of successful integration into Australian society, in which Muslims are found to share values relating to democracy and liberalism.[14] There are also, however, some high profile legal cases regarding Islam that provide a different view.[15] While the idea of multiculturalism as a social policy tends to focus on culture, a more acid test arises with legal pluralism. Competing legal traditions necessarily raise more acute difficulties than cultural pluralism, as the former bring the nature of sovereignty into play.

The paradox is that, although interfaith and inter-cultural

marriage are taken as the typical indicators of successful integration, they also represent the dilution of community identity. For that reason, most orthodox religious traditions resist interfaith or inter-cultural marriage. The classic example is ultra-orthodox Hasidic Jews of New York, but the same arguments apply to Australian Jews and Muslims—in fact to any closed community.[16] In the United Kingdom, the general consensus is that post-war migration produced a system of parallel communities. In Australia, as elsewhere, the rise of right-wing militancy and the growth of Islamophobia have brought into question our sense of multicultural success.

There is clearly evidence of Islamophobia in modern Australia alongside rising antisemitism. One in ten Australians display strong feelings of Islamophobia. At the same time, while Muslims have educational levels similar to the host population, they lag behind in employment, income levels, and home ownership. However, a considerable body of recent research by Professor Riaz Hassan,[17] from the International Centre for Muslim and non-Muslim Understanding at the University of South Australia, provides an encouraging picture of religious diversity. He employs the idea of social distance from the work of the American sociologist Emory Bogardus, which postulates that our sense of nearness or distance from other members of society can be quantified in terms of affect (and which has a very different meaning from the requirement of 'social distancing' in the current crisis). In general terms, Australians do not express or experience a sense of social distance from Muslims. In response to the question, "Would I live in a place where there are Muslims?", 46% agreed. On another measure, 17% of Australians felt completely comfortable having a Muslim as a close friend. It is also important to recognise that the majority of Muslims define themselves as Australian. In the 2016 census, almost 70% of Muslims nominated 'Australian' as their national identity. Hassan's general conclusion is that Australian Muslims are "young city dwellers, who are optimistic about life in Australia, they are bringing up children, enrolling in higher education, and embracing the English language and an Australian identity."[18]

These results are important in correcting popular misunderstanding about Muslim communities in Australia. One popular anxiety regarding Muslim fertility rates is based on factually correct information. The standardised fertility rate for Muslim women was 2.5, whereas for Christian women it was 2.1. The Muslim community has indeed grown rapidly. In 1966, there were 200,885 Muslims in Australia, and by 2016, there were 604,200 or an increase of 200%. By 2050, it is anticipated that there will be one and a half million Muslims. These growth figures feed into the ideology of extremism. In this connection, we have to recognise the growth of political extremist groups that reject multiculturalism, migrants, Muslim communities, and various forms of liberalism such as gender equality. One underlying fear is the actual replacement of the white population by Muslims. A key figure in this claim is the French intellectual, Renaud Camus, the author of *La Grand Remplacement*,[19] who argues that white populations with low fertility rates are being slowly replaced by Muslim communities with high fertility rates. Camus claims that his ideas were first inspired by Enoch Powell's speech on the rivers of blood. These ideas have gone global. For example, Brenton Tarrant, the perpetrator of the New Zealand terror attack in 2019, also cited the theory of population replacement in his manifesto. The notion that migrants in general and Muslims in particular are replacing national white community is explored extensively by the British political theorist, Eric Kaufmann, in *Whiteshift: Populism, Immigration and the Future of White Majorities*.[20] These are arguments that have been challenged as factually inaccurate and for employing demography as an instrument of racism.[21] Although it is true that over time Muslim fertility rates are equal to host populations, demographers often speak about the 'second demographic transition' as Western populations are shrinking and ageing. For contemporary demography, this population trend cannot be reversed *without* inward migration.[22]

Aboriginal Australia is also part of the story of our social diversity, but it is not part of the story of multiculturalism. Aboriginal people are the first people not the latecomers. In fact, our relationship to Australian Aboriginal communities and culture further disrupts the lucky-country narrative. It is well known that in terms of mortality and morbidity Aboriginal people fall far behind non-indigenous Australians. Health data for the period 2010-2012 show that the life expectancy for Aboriginal males was 69.1 against 79.7 for non-indigenous men. The mortality rate for Aboriginal and Torres Strait Islander people under five years in 2003 was 11.6 per 1000. However, there have been improvements in Aboriginal health partly as a consequence of the *Closing the Gap* health policy of the Council of Australian Governments in 2008. Child mortality fell from 104.4 over 100,000 in 2008 to 73.2 over 100,000 in 2016. Nevertheless, diabetes, blindness, and drug dependency remain critical health problems within the Aboriginal community.

In modern times, there have been two legal and symbolic changes in the relationship between Aboriginal peoples and Australian society. The Mabo decision in 1992 rejected the myth of *terra nullius*, by which British colonialists claimed possession of an empty land and created a sovereign state and private property, thereby denying Aboriginal entitlement to the land. The Apology or Sorry Day in 1998 was a significant landmark occasion in the journey towards recognition and reconciliation. However, ongoing debates about further changes to the Constitution along with recognition of Aboriginal customary law have not produced definite advances for Aboriginal people. Their marginalisation in Australia and their sense of injustice are strong indications of unresolved issues, and their morbidity and mortality figures continue to give a clear message of exclusion from mainstream Australia.

In terms of the recognition of Aboriginal religion and spiritual life, the closure of Uluru to tourists on 25 October 2019 was generally welcomed as recognition of traditional ownership and the sacredness of the rock itself. For many generations of Australians, Ayers Rock (now known as Uluru) has been a major tourist attraction and Pauline Hanson, the One Nation leader, compared the recognition of native demands to Uluru to closing Sydney's Bondi Beach—both should be available to citizens. Other critics pointed out that Uluru was in fact an intrinsic feature of the National Park and therefore belongs to everyone. Recognising Aboriginal spirituality in a secular democracy may be less onerous and challenging to the citizenry than any substantial redistribution of land and recognition of Aboriginal law.

The closure went without significant incident, but it does, nevertheless, bring into view the ongoing tensions between secular citizenship and the historic rights of Aboriginal people to restitution, return of the land to its traditional owners, and recognition of their sacred traditions. It also demonstrates that Aboriginal rights fall outside the claims of multiculturalism. They cannot be seen in the same category as the rights of migrant Greeks and Italians, for example. However, the precise nature of their legal status in terms of international law is complex. For example, in theoretical and legal terms, it is difficult to place Aboriginal rights in relation to the rights of stateless peoples and national minorities.[23]

The issue of Aboriginal rights brings us to the more general question of citizenship. Looking at the recent history of citizenship, early discussions of social or welfare citizenship have expanded to consider notions of multicultural citizenship and differential citizenship. These more refined ideas about citizenship—especially the status of Aboriginal peoples and migrant minorities—have been driven by the Canadian experience. The key publication was Will Kymlicka's *Multicultural Citizenship*.[24] My own view is that while comparisons between Canada and Australia are appropriate, we have to recognise two important differences. One is the separate cultural and linguistic history of Quebec. The second is that Aboriginal people in Canada such as the Cree nation straddle the Canadian and American border.

Political theorists argue that Australian citizenship has been conceived in narrow legal or state terms, and there is no substantive notion of citizenship in the Constitution. Even in the Nationality and Citizenship Act of 1948, the main issue was how to include aliens into citizenship. As late as the 1990s, the main concern was how to turn 'New Australians' into bona fide citizens. However, "Substantive conceptions of citizenship were also promoted by Australian churches, both Protestant and Catholic. Nonetheless, our heritage in the area of citizenship leaves much work to be done."[25]

In terms of international standards of citizenship and human rights, treatment of Aboriginal peoples raises ongoing questions about Australia's ranking in human rights terms. In many ways, the treatment of boat people is more problematic than the failure to resolve the place of Aboriginals in a modern democracy in terms of human rights according to our ranking by the United Nations. Off-shore holding of refugees and asylum seekers has led to widespread criticism of Australian policies.

The role of Christian missions is also part of the history of Australian settlement. Christian missionary activity has received national and international criticism for removing Aboriginal children from their communities to be educated in church schools. This issue became very public through the release of the film *The Rabbit-Proof Fence* (2002), which was based on the true story of three Aboriginal girls who escaped from the missions in 1931 and set off across the outback in search of their communities. There is debate about whether these educational policies in fact constituted (cultural) genocide, but it is difficult to escape that conclusion. The definition of genocide is perhaps confused by the introduction of specific intention as a criterion. In legal terms, it is necessary to prove that the perpetrators had a clear intention to destroy a people and their culture. The question of intentionality is perhaps less important than the simple fact that missionary education destroyed their cultural legacy without effectively equipping Aboriginals to live successfully in a secular Australian urban society.

Leaving for now the question of social diversity and in attempting to understand the relationship between religion and democracy, we need to address the question of secularisation. In the second half of the last century, the general assumption was that secularisation was an inevitable feature of modernisation. The key figure was the Oxford sociologist and Fellow of All Souls College, Bryan Wilson, whose *Religion in Secular Society* was a key text.[26] He demonstrated that, for British society in particular, the churches were in decline, recruitment to the ministry was shrinking, and the social and political influence of the churches was limited. He recognised that the situation of religion in the United States was different. While the churches were booming, he claimed that they enjoyed success but at the cost of their contents. To take one example, the mega church is indicative of vibrant growth, but such churches pay more attention to providing social services rather than delivering the Christian message. The supply-side theory of religion which I have already discussed was one criticism of Wilson's contrast between the British and American experience. American religion was booming because of the efficiency of the religious market. This view was also challenged by the idea of public religions (Solidarity in Poland; Latin American liberation theology; the Iranian Shia Revolution; the American Moral Majority) in José Casanova's *Public Religions in the*

Modern World.[27] Another American sociologist, Peter L. Berger, had originally accepted the idea of inevitable secularisation in *The Sacred Canopy*,[28] in which the ancient pillars of religion were being eroded and a market of competing religious views and options had emerged. He came to revise his views, when he reversed his original argument in *The Desecularization of the World. Resurgent Religion and World Politics*.[29] He presented a simple fact. While Western Europe could be defined as largely secular, this was not true of the rest of the world, especially in Africa, where Christianity was growing rapidly. Islamic reform and revitalisation were also counterexamples.

Sociologists have also pointed to the global spread of Pentecostalism, which has challenged the traditional dominance of Roman Catholicism, especially in Latin America. David Lehmann, whose original research was into Chilean politics and landownership, published *Struggle for the Spirit: Religious Transformation and Popular Culture in Brazil and Latin America*,[30] which examines religious growth in its diverse forms in the South American continent. Other writers see the vibrant growth of Pentecostalism as a movement parallel to early Methodism.[31] Both Methodism and Pentecostalism are seen as movements that have attracted the poor and the deserted to religious faith. Although Pentecostalism is often seen as a challenge to Catholicism, many Catholic liturgical services now contain elements borrowed from Pentecostalism and other evangelical forms of Christianity. Charismatic Catholicism is another illustration of these developments. In more general terms, we should attend to the consequences of Vatican II to understand how the Church has responded to modernity, political liberalism, and a more secular world.

Thus, in opposition to the standard secularisation theories of the last century, in contemporary sociology of religion there is a growing view that, while the mainstream churches are in decline, the growth of individual spirituality, online religion, bar churches, and dinner churches suggest that the demand for a religious identity and spiritual comfort are widespread, especially among younger generations. The growth of a digital culture with new technologies is changing religious practice and belief.[32]

These developments also have important consequences, not just for Christian communities. Online discussion of Shari'a among Muslim communities has encouraged what is known as online 'Sharia shopping', whereby individual Muslims can eventually find the Shari'a interpretation they want. In general terms, online debates about religion, moral teaching, and norms of everyday behaviour raise questions about the traditional authority of all forms of religious leadership and traditional values.

How can we interpret these religious developments? I argue, in line with de Tocqueville, that religious individualism is secularisation involving the loss of religious communalism as a basis of civil society. Individuals can find friendship and virtual membership online, but can these forms of belonging ever replace community membership based on the parish and the local church? If the churches have been among the main pillars of civil society, then their decline must have negative consequences for civil life. We can recognise that online or digital religion or simply religion on TV have benefits for elderly or disabled people who cannot physically attend church services. However, the longer-term consequences of new forms of religious individualism are not especially encouraging. These developments are more pronounced in America than elsewhere. My classes on religion in New York typically contained students who practised witchcraft (in Central Park), Zen Buddhism, paganism, veganism, and shamanism, alongside evangelical born-again Christians from the Mississippi and liberal Jews from Brooklyn. While supply-side theories interpret such diversity as religious health, in my view this is the neoliberal market in religious garb. In conclusion, we may not have Wilson-style secularisation. What we have instead is individualistic and privatised forms of religion, and the growth of DIY hybrid religiosity or "hyper-real religions".[33] These developments are connected to the erosion of communal patterns of society and growth of online communication. There is a long tradition of political thought, at least from de Tocqueville onwards, that saw the solidarity of civil society and citizenship as the basis of a functional democracy.

Another aspect of this issue—social solidarity—is the slow decline of rural Australia with the drift of population, especially young people, to the city for employment. The shift of populations to the large cities—most notably Melbourne and Sydney—underlines the significance of this social and economic change. The decline of the rural church has followed the economic decline of rural Australia.[34] The outback is an important foundation of Australian culture and self-understanding. It was the locus of mateship as a basis for important values such as trust, mutual respect, and equality. The idea of mateship has been criticised for its historical gender bias reflecting a world of unchallenged patriarchy, but it can be defended for promoting mutual respect and shared responsibility. Mateship was one component of the Lucky Country, but it has been challenged by feminist movements. Early feminists were active in such movements and societies as the Victorian Women's Suffrage Society, which was launched in 1848 and was part of a broader network of early feminists. Prominent activists at the time included Henrietta Dugdale. As a secular radical, she condemned religion for the abuses suffered by women. Like other secularists, she blamed religion for hypocrisy and superstition. To the criticism of religion, she included problems associated with male dominance. Radical women of the time advocated for divorce reform, improvements in conditions at work, the need for equal pay, and legal reform to protect women from domestic violence.[35] Although feminists may argue that little has changed, we cannot ignore the political and legal success of #MeToo. As of writing this essay, Harvey Weinstein has been sentenced to twenty-three years in prison for multiple charges of sexual abuse and rape charges. The verdict is regarded as a landmark in the growth of the #MeToo movement.

The erosion of mateship—for good or for bad—is one dimension of the decline of the outback in connection with the industrialisation of agriculture, in which the small farm cannot survive the competitive pressure on prices from large retailers such as Coles and Woolworths. The low price of a bottle of milk is a good indicator of the pressure on small holdings. If catastrophic bushfires, as witnessed in 2019-2020, become a regular feature of the Australian summer, then the decline of small rural communities will gather apace and with them the historical component of Australian self-understanding. The rural church will disappear along with the rural community and the values to which they gave birth.

I have placed considerable importance for both religion and democracy on community. We can consider a broad cluster of C-words: citizenship; civility; civilisation; and courtesy as a fundamental component of political theory. They are highly interconnected both linguistically and historically. There is an established view in sociology and political theory that civility certainly refers to good manners and considerate behaviour. It includes a set of norms for kindly behaviour towards the elderly and the frail. It typically promotes respect for others. It is also important in respect for difference. Perhaps more fundamental is the idea that civility underpins dialogue and debate. This idea was fundamental to the work of the American sociologist Edward Shils who, writing in the context of McCarthyism, argued that without civility there could not be effective debate and discussion, and asked, "How can a democracy function without these?"[36] Declining civility spells out declining democracy. One argument against the sociology of civility is that the very idea is culturally specific. Chinese have Confucius; Muslims have the *adab* literature defining pious behaviour; we have Erasmus, who did in fact produce one of the earliest accounts of good behaviour in a book critical of boys' bad behaviour—*De civilitate morum puerilium* (1530). It was an instant success being translated into English by Robert Whittington in 1532, under the title *A Little Book of Good Manners in Children*.[37] Religion is not the only basis for good behaviour but it is certainly important as a source of norms for respect and care for the other. Again, returning to Kenneth Dempsey's research into rural Australia (with special emphasis on Methodism), he found that laypeople had little interest in theology as such and saw the benefit of religion as teaching their children good manners, respect for others, and decency. With the decline of religion, is there evidence of a decline of civility in Australia? Consider the behaviour of politicians in parliamentary debate; think of abusive behaviour on public transport, especially at night time; take into account the claims of women in #MeToo regarding abuse from men in privileged social positions; or a relatively trivial issue such as ball tampering in cricket, which produced a national outcry.

In the study of civility, are we always looking downwards at children, at the working class, at outsiders? In modern societies, is incivility not also characteristic of the elite, such as Donald Trump's attitude towards women? One Australian example comes from the Royal Commission into Misconduct in the Banking, Superannuation and Financial Services Industry (2019), which found extensive evidence of bankers engaging in fraud, bad practice, greed, and mistreatment of clients such as selling insurance to customers who were dead. One conclusion was that senior managers through wealth, status, and residential addresses were remote from the everyday world of customers and ordinary citizens and could treat them with disrespect, or in my terms with incivility. Incivility has often been associated with the working class or, in contemporary terms, 'the chavs' (young people of low education, low culture, and bad behaviour).[38] In the contemporary world, incivility is increasing associated with elites and indeed with royalty.[39]

The decline of democracy and civility can be seen in terms of long-term historical transformations, but there are also rapid and unexpected transitions. For example, since the financial crisis of 2008-2011, there have been major social and economic problems: austerity packages and rising inequality; unaffordable housing; children living with parents because they are unable to raise a mortgage; the growth of the gig labour market (short contracts, no pensions, no health care, no prospects); rising house prices; erosion of pensions; and income inequality. While these economic and social problems are not in fact recent developments, they have been intensified in connection with what is often called "the financialisation of capitalism."[40]

The impact of these changes falls heavily on young men with no college education and no history of continuous employment. In the United States, morbidity and mortality rates for non-Hispanic white males are revealing—a decline in life expectancy for the first time in decades.[41] The result at least in the United States is rising political extremism, populism, and the politics of President Trump. The most interesting development has been the rise of groups such as InCel—involuntary celibacy.[42] In the radical discourse of masculinity, young women have too much power; men need to assert their authority over women and receive more respect from society. Violent populism appears to be associated with such movements.

The oddity of such developments, on the surface, is the support from organized religion for Donald Trump. Evangelicals and

Liberal societies in a religious world

Catholics both support him on account of his stances on abortion and Israel.[43] Trump's right-wing populism receives support from increased numbers of Jews given his "plan for Palestine" and his attitude towards Israel. He receives support from Catholics who rightly believe he supports their views on a range of issues: the traditional family, pro-life politics, and education. Evangelical Christians are attracted to Trump because they feel vulnerable in terms of race and religion.[44] The core issue among American Evangelicals is the need to ban abortion and reverse *Roe v Wade*. The Evangelical argument is that men and women are different. Men are patriarchs in the private and the public world. The role of women is in the home to nurture their children and to support their family. Evangelical activism in the United States brings into focus our understanding of the separation of church and state, and how sexism and misogyny are embedded within a democratic culture.[45]

The early forms of populism emerged in the United States in the 1860s but contemporary interest in populism dates from the financial crisis of 2008-2011, the austerity policies that followed, and the dramatic political manifestations of it in Brexit and movements against migrants in Europe and the United States. Most accounts of populism have little to say about religion or about the intellectuals whose publications and speeches provide much of the content of populist ideology. Sociologists have taken note of the fact that, in response to the refugee crisis and Angela Merkel's response, Europe's cultural and political boundaries have been defined (ambiguously) in terms of either Christianity or Judeo-Christianity. Eastern Orthodoxy is equally critical of ethnic diversity but also of Western moral decay. The idea of *Das Abendland*—the romantic idea of the land of setting sun—has been resurrected.[46] Many accounts of populism treat its followers as illiterate and stupid, the left-behind or the deplorables. We need to take seriously the impact of intellectuals of various religious persuasions on populist ideas, ranging from such figures as Enoch Powell (a staunch Anglican),

33

Sir Roger Scruton (the English conservative),[47] Renaud Camus (the French intellectual, author of *Le grand replacement*, and founder of National Council of European Resistance), Benjamin Harnwell (the founder of Dignitatis Humanae Institute), to Steve Bannon, the early intellectual force behind Trump's election strategy and influential force in the Academy for the Judeo-Christian West in Rome. These intellectuals oppose multiculturalism, social diversity, and cultural difference as causes of secularisation and European decline. For Camus, the problem of Europe's decline—both political and cultural—arises from what he regards as a "replacist totalitarianism."

The development of populism, political radicalism, and Christian conservatism may be less obvious in Australia than in the United States. However, Pauline Hanson is and remains a controversial figure having started a radical conservative party—One Nation. The movement Reclaim Australia has a small but vociferous following and has staged rallies against migration and Islam. Islamophobia is widespread in Australia.[48] The terrorist attack on mosques in Christchurch, New Zealand, in March 2019 was undertaken by Brenton Tarrant—a white supremacist and a supporter of 'alt-right'—from Grafton, New South Wales. Demonstrating the globalisation of terrorism, in his manifesto he refers to the "Great Displacement" namely, the decline of white population and its replacement by Muslim immigrants who have much higher fertility rates than national white populations.

While these terrorist developments are clearly not supported by Christians, there is widespread anxiety among Christian conservatives, for example about family life. The Family First party (2002-2017) was most active in South Australia, where it was supported by Pentecostalists and smaller Christian churches. It promoted respect for the family, traditional values, and the Christian faith.[49] The relationship between men and women, the role of the family, traditional Christian values, assumptions about education, and so forth have been challenged and are changing. Ann Summers, in *Damned Whores and God's Police*,[50] contributed to the rewriting of Australian history and specifically attitudes towards the role of women in public life. 'Hegemonic masculinity',[51] domestic abuse, and violence towards women are thought to be on the increase in Australia—the brutal murder of Hannah Clarke and her three children by her estranged husband in Brisbane in February 2020 being only one incident in a recent string of similar cases. Violence surrounding masculinity and far right movements has now become a general problem in Western democracies. Christian conservatism is non-violent, but its traditional values—defence of the family and traditional patriarchy—overlap with alt-right values and conservative politics.

In these radical changes to Australian society, are the churches on the back foot? Although church and state have always been in some degree of conflict, they can both be regarded as disciplining institutions over society. However, in contemporary society, the state often appears to regulate or discipline churches by claiming authority over their practices and institutions. In many respects, the churches are subject to governance by the state.[52] The modern state has often taken aggressive action towards Scientology. While it has been regarded as a religion in Australia since the 1950s, it is regarded as a cult in France. In many areas we find church and state at loggerheads over the confidentiality of the confession, same-sex marriage, the definition of marriage, the role and contents of religion in schools, the right of religious schools to reject teachers who are gay, and the future possibility of declaring circumcision an unlawful practice on young boys. The legal struggle over same-sex marriage exposed the depth of division in Australia between young and old, Christians and secularists, and tradition and modernity.[53] Taking a long historical view, the Christian tradition about the family and sexual identity is unambiguous. Marriage and family life did not play a large role in the theology of St Augustine, but the biblical message against sodomy is fundamentally clear. In the Protestant Reformation, Luther railed against what he saw as the corrupt practices of Rome's priesthood. Sodomy was clearly a sin. Although liberal Christians and secular Australians welcomed the passage of the Marriage Amendment Act in December 2017 with 61.6% of the general population in favour, we can only draw two conclusions. It was an Act that contradicted what had been the basic understanding of the Christian churches for generations and it was an Act to bring the churches into line with secular society. The law in service of the state was also increasingly determined to support people who claimed to be victims of sexual abuse from priests. The most serious case that illustrates the principle was the charge against His Eminence George Cardinal Pell for offences against boys in Ballarat and Melbourne in 2019-20. The Cardinal was eventually acquitted on 7 April 2020, when the High Court of Australia concluded that the alleged rape was "possible, but not reasonably possible."

Perhaps these developments might produce a new definition of a secular society in which the state exercises governance over what can count as 'a religion' and what is acceptable or unacceptable as 'religious behaviour'.

Given the various challenges to Australian life, is Australia a lucky country? What are the ingredients of successful societies? Are we a happy people?[54] There is a well-established connection between democratic responsible government, individual freedoms, and individual happiness. Most of the countries in the world that rank highest in overall satisfaction with life have been successful democracies for more than eighty years.[55] Generally speaking, these societies also have functional welfare states. Thus, in terms of life satisfaction, it is perhaps not surprising that the highest ranked societies are Denmark, Finland, Switzerland, the Netherlands, and Sweden. Three countries with a history of Westminster-style democracies and sound economies, namely Australia, Canada, and New Zealand, are also highly ranked.[56] In world happiness surveys, such as the United Nations' *World Happiness Survey*,[57] 'optimal societies' enjoy stability over time, high productivity of goods and services, realisation of national ideals, and demonstrable levels of 'liveability' as measured by health and life satisfaction.

Are religious people in modern society happier or more successful than secular people? Unfortunately, the sociological and psychological evidence provides no unambiguous or consistent findings. Research on social capital in the United States found that religiosity correlates well with life satisfaction or happiness, but these findings might be explained by the social relationships that are supported by church activities and communal bonds. For example, families that pray together stay together, and that bonding—rather than faith—specifically supports happiness. In psychological research, those investigations using the Oxford Happiness Inventory found religiosity to be consistently associated with happiness, whereas the Depression-Happiness Scale consistently found no association. Despite the methodological sophistication, some psychologists, such as Michael Argyle, have concluded that, from a psychological point of view, we have no coherent theory of happiness. However, we might want to try to differentiate between religious traditions in Christianity rather than treating the Christian churches as all singing from the same hymn sheet. The famous German sociologist, Max Weber (1864 – 1920), in his two essays on *The Protestant Ethic* and *The Spirit of Capitalism*, argued that Calvinism presented believers with a severe psychological dilemma. Because the world and our lives within it was predetermined by God, neither faith nor good works guarantees salvation. In simple terms, no believing Calvinist could have any certainty that they were saved. Weber argued that, over time, Calvinists came to accept the idea that success in this world (such as the accumulation of wealth) was a proxy measure of salvation. This psychological and theological conundrum was one cultural cause of the rise of capitalism. Weber also recognised that his Calvinistic route contrasts with the history of Methodism. Weber drew attention to these emotional elements in the piety of the Herrnhut Brotherhood and Methodism, which softened the Calvinistic message of predestinarian fate. Wesley's Arminian theology preached salvation for all. Wesley had a clear view that love of God was the fountain of human happiness. In his old age, at a meeting in Dublin with Irish Methodists, he declared, "You are made to be happy in God".[58] The hymns of his brother, Charles Wesley, celebrated the happiness of the faithful Christian in this world in the company of Jesus as lord and saviour. Wesley's message is compelling. If the pious are not happy in their lives, for what reason did Christ die on the Cross? The message of Paul was short and emphatic: Christ is risen.[59] The message for democracy is less clear and emphatic. Functional democracies are more likely to be happy successful societies, but there are many indications that modern democracies are failing.

Democratic leaders in a religious world

Damien T. Freeman

"I T IS ALL THIS THING called love," a Fingo elder told the Commission on Native Law and Custom in South Africa in 1883, "We do not understand it at all. This thing called love has been introduced."[1] Such incomprehension about the introduction of romantic love into Fingo society was part of the misfortune of European colonisation. We easily forget what it was about Western ways that was so incomprehensible to the indigenous population. Traditional leaders in a colonial world had to struggle with new and incomprehensible things like love if they were to retain the confidence of their people, for whom such ideas suddenly became an important part of how they lived their lives.

We take it for granted that love is a fundamental feature of the human world. Indeed, "the love is the same", we were told solemnly in recent years when being encouraged to abandon the traditional definition of marriage. But this thing we call love has not always been the same, and our commitment to romantic love, C. S. Lewis reminds us, "has erected impassable barriers between us and the classical past or the oriental present".[2] Lewis is introducing the courtly love of the troubadours, which he explains is itself a development of a misunderstanding of the ironic humour of Ovid, who assumes that his audience will know that love is really a frivolous subject for literature, and so will appreciate the irony of his mock solemnity. Yet this thing we call love, which, it seems to us, is a natural thing to regard as a noble and ennobling passion, is not as natural a feature of human experience as it might at first seem: "it is only if we imagine ourselves trying to explain this doctrine to Aristotle, Virgil, St Paul, or the author of *Beowulf*, that we become aware how far from natural it is."[3] So the love that Australia's democratic political leaders came to understand is now the same has not always been the same. This should remind us that we are sometimes wilfully ignorant both of how unnatural some of our most prized concepts are to others, and, in turn, how incomprehensible are other ways of life to us. Thus, it should come as no surprise that democratic leaders might struggle as much as tribal elders to comprehend categories foreign to their own worldview.

The British politician and philosopher, Jesse Norman, reminds us that "leadership begins in respect for the social order, and so in modesty. It pushes leaders towards a close study of their people, all the people, and their institutions."[4] In saying this, he affirms advice that was given over three centuries earlier by his predecessor, Edmund Burke, who wrote that "The temper of the people amongst whom he presides ought . . . to be the first study of a statesman."[5] The political leader needs to understand the values and institutions of all the people who comprise the nation in order to develop effective domestic policy. It is no less important, however, for the political leader, as diplomat, to understand the values and institutions of the people who comprise the international community, if he or she is to develop effective foreign policy.

One source of social order that the aspiring leader would do well to study is religion. A religion has a powerful sway over the formation of values in its individual adherents. Religion also has a tenacious capacity to bind adherents together into communities of faith. Religion may not be the only source of value or the only force binding communities together, but it has been an important one—at least historically. Indeed, for a long time it was believed that social cohesion required uniform religious adherence, and difference in religious practice or belief was associated with social division and disorder.

That a leader needs to understand the people in order to govern them leaves open the possibility that, having made a special study of the people, the leader could reach the conclusion that the best way of governing the people is by repressing them. A special study of their values and institutions—including religious ones—might enable the leader to determine the most effective course for repressing them without too much resistance. In a democratic state, this is not an option, however, as the leader requires the consent of the governed. That at least means that the leader ought not be able to repress the majority in a democratic state, even if the leader might, through a close study of the majority of the people, draw the conclusion that their support could be secured through policies that repress a minority of the population, or at least that a majoritarian mandate would not be compromised by adopting policies that affect a minority adversely.

In a state that regards itself as a liberal democracy, even this possibility ought to be extinguished by a conviction that the liberty of the entire population matters. Thus, in a liberal democracy, a system of checks and balances is required to ensure that the interests of people are not unreasonably repressed, even if these people's support is not required for the sake of a democratic mandate. At least since Federation, Australia has prided itself on being a liberal democracy—even if there is some disagreement about its record as such. So political leadership in Australia is going to require a close study of all the Australian people, and the values and institutions that animate them—both those that enjoy broad support across the Australian population, and those that animate different sections of the population.

Historically, Australia has been regarded as a Christian country. How deeply Christianity became rooted in the country is debatable, and so the extent to which Australians were ever animated by Christianity might well be limited. A majority of Australians (some 67% of the population) still regarded themselves as Christians of one denomination or another, however, for the purpose of the 2011 census. The Pew Research Center's 2015 report predicts that the world at large will become more religious by 2050, whereas Australia will become less religious.[6] By 2050, it is predicted that over 40% of Australians will not adhere to any religion (and only 47% of Australians will adhere to any Christian denomination), whereas an increased majority of the global population will adhere to either Islam or Christianity (up from a combined 54% in 2010 to 61% in 2050). A similar trend to that in Australia is predicted in the United Kingdom and New Zealand, but not in the United States, where it is predicted that over 60% of the population will still adhere to Christianity. This means that the Australian situation will be at odds both with the situation in the United States, which will remain predominantly Christian, and the world at large, which will become increasingly Christian and Muslim.

This creates two challenges for democratic leaders in Australia. On the one hand, they might struggle to comprehend the significance of religion for what will become a minority of Australians. In a liberal democratic state, it will remain important to accommodate such a minority, however incomprehensible their form of life might be to the majority. On the other hand, Australian leaders might struggle to comprehend the significance of religion within the world at large. If religion assumes a greater significance—

for better or worse—in the community of nations, it will remain important for the international relations of a non-religious country that its leaders can navigate its way in a world in which the religious commitments of other increasingly religious countries are increasingly incomprehensible to the democratic leaders of that non-religious country.

What would it mean for the religious world to be incomprehensible to non-religious lawmakers and non-religious diplomats? There are at least five basic commitments that are part of a religious worldview, and which might be incomprehensible to someone with a non-religious worldview.

The first is a conviction that an adequate worldview must include some account of the transcendent. This carries with it the conviction that any purely materialist worldview—the theory that nothing exists except matter and its movements and modifications—would ultimately be inadequate as an account of the world we live in. Competing religious worldviews might disagree about the nature of the transcendent, but they would agree that an adequate worldview would need to include some account of this.

Secondly, a religious worldview usually entails a commitment to some form of the idea that metaphysics dictates ethics. This means that, ultimately, understanding how human beings should live involves having recourse to some fact about ultimate reality. This carries with it the conviction that any relativistic approach to ethics would ultimately be inadequate.

The third idea that might be incomprehensible is the conviction that the nature of reality is such that it imposes upon all of us—or at least some of us—obligations that we cannot renounce.

Connected to this idea that ethical life is anchored in ultimate reality, and that an account of ultimate reality involves an account of the transcendent, is the fourth idea, namely that the transcendent manifests in the human world through institutions. This carries with it the conviction that any account of what it is to be human cannot be given in terms of *the individual* alone, rather than in terms of people living together—*the individual in community*—as the most basic unit for thinking about what is fundamental to being human.

Finally, there is a conviction that the quest at the heart of human flourishing is not for the individual to find personal meaning in a meaningless universe, but to discover the meaning inherent in the world and to act accordingly.

Different religions and different religious denominations will, of course, disagree about these matters, but they will share some basic convictions about the nature of reality and morality. It is these shared convictions that might prove incomprehensible to people with non-religious worldviews. The challenge then arises for political leaders in Australia, who are increasingly likely to have non-religious worldviews, and who seek the support of the majority of an increasingly non-religious Australian electorate, to study the values of religious people and their institutions, which are at risk of becoming increasingly incomprehensible to non-religious democratic leaders and their peoples.

This risk is brought into sharp relief by a retired Justice of the High Court of Australia, J. D. Heydon QC, who has warned that the "modern elites" are introducing a new form of tyranny in their quest for "tolerance."[7] He begins by introducing the "elite of the Federation generation" and reflecting on their deference to religious authority. They are contrasted with the "modern elites", who, he suggests, seek to exclude any role for religion in Australian public discussion. Two recent incidents are discussed, which Heydon says exemplify the modern elites' transition from indifference to religion to a form of anti-clericalism. Drawing on Peter Kurti's *The Tyranny of Tolerance*, Heydon suggests that the modern elites' tendency towards anti-clericalism has not only allowed them to associate themselves with a failure to appeal to reason. Their demands for "tolerance" are revealed to be demands for "unconditional surrender" and unconditional acceptance of their chosen creeds. In making such demands, it is argued that they overlook the role of courtesy and reason in public discourse and civil society. Heydon says their creed embodies a modern ideal of liberalism, in which there is neither a place for persuasion of those with whom one disagrees, nor tolerance of them. As a form of secular liberalism, the modern elites' creed is shown to have its origin in Christianity, by reference to Sir Larry Siedentop's *Inventing the Individual*, which traces the roots of liberalism back to values revealed by the advent of Christ. And yet, Heydon claims, the modern elites not only despise and seek to marginalise the Christian religion that introduced the notions of the inherent value and fundamental equality of all human beings, which are central to any form of liberalism, but they go further in rejecting the cultural tradition of Christianity. Although Heydon concedes that the exercise of public power by the legislature and the judiciary has not yet significantly threatened the interests of religious people and their institutions, he suggests that the modern elites might soon resort to the force of law. He concludes with the admonition that, although for the time being it is only through conduct such as bullying and ridicule that the elites seek to prevent public expression of religion, this might be a sign of darker times to come.

Heydon is correct to draw a contrast between the attitudes of Australian political leaders in the late nineteenth and early twenty-first centuries. Humility and gratitude for blessings have given way to a preoccupation with rights and entitlements. The leaders' attitudes to religion at the time of Federation is, however, more nuanced. As the Jesuit lawyer, Frank Brennan, has shown, several of the key politicians did not necessarily have a personal reverence for any organized religion.[8] What they did have, however, is a practical imperative for showing reverence to God. This was because they believed that it would be easier to carry the vote of the sections of the population who took religious adherence seriously if the preamble to the act establishing the new Commonwealth recited that the people relied upon the blessing of Almighty God. What this suggests is that, although it may be correct to draw attention to changes in the leaders' personal worldviews over the last century, it is perhaps even more important to draw attention to their perception of practical political imperatives.

Heydon made his comments in 2017, at the time when the Commonwealth Government was conducting a postal survey about changing the definition of marriage according to Australian law. It is worth noting that some religious communities expressed concern that their interests were not being taken seriously during this debate. A number of these communities were located in marginal seats, and in the wake of the 2019 federal election, both the government and the opposition finally came to see that these communities felt they had been neglected, and that this had influenced how they voted.[9] Leaders of all political colours were quick to realise that there is a political cost to failing to take these people's concerns seriously. They calculated that there was now a practical imperative for them to engage seriously with the concerns of those with a religious worldview because that is what political leaders do: they find a way to overcome such incomprehensibility when needs must.

When Queen Elizabeth I came to the throne, she returned England to the Protestant faith established by her father, Henry VIII, and from which the realm had departed temporarily, during her sister's reign, when Mary I had restored the

Catholic faith in England. Elizabeth's decision had not only theological consequences, but political, military, and commercial implications. In particular, once England was isolated from Catholic Europe, Elizabeth needed to look beyond Christendom for trade partners. This meant establishing cordial relations with the Moroccan king, the Persian shah, and the Ottoman sultan, all of which she achieved very successfully. It was an achievement that was short-lived, however. After Elizabeth's death, she was succeeded by James VI of Scotland, who was keen to restore England's relationship with Catholic Europe. Once the Wars of Religion in Europe had passed, there was no practical need for Protestant England to maintain commercial and strategic relations with the Islamic world. In consequence, England fell back into old attitudes to Islam.

This footnote to history is picked up by a British Renaissance scholar, Jerry Brotton, who points out the conflicting ways in which Elizabeth's alliances with Morocco, Persia, and the Ottoman Empire were seen by her subjects: "For many English Catholics and Puritans, these alliances were an abomination, but to a number of statesmen and merchants they represented profit and possibility."[10] Elizabeth managed these domestic tensions in a way that overcame incomprehension of Islam, but only to the extent necessary for commerce and strategic partnership:

> This does not mean that England under Elizabeth was a halcyon world where Christians and Muslims happily coexisted in an atmosphere of religious toleration and acceptance of each other's cultural differences. The relationship was often based on mutual suspicion, misunderstanding and ambivalence. Its consequences were various and sometimes contradictory. Those involved were mostly driven by self-interest and did not believe they were playing out some profound clash between civilisations. It is a subtle and complicated history that illuminates the Elizabethan period, and

also our own.[11]

That an "amicable relationship" between Protestant England and the Islamic countries prospered under Elizabeth, Brotton explains, "arose not from a principle of tolerance but as a result of political expediency." Elizabeth was motivated by practical necessity, and for this reason, such goodwill as there was lasted only as long as the practical necessity lasted.* Fast forward four hundred years, if there is no clear practical need for democratic leaders to overcome their incomprehension of religious people and their commitments, it is hardly surprising that incomprehension might be the order of the day. The relationship between Elizabethan England and the Islamic world "emerged out of a very specific set of circumstances during the European Reformation . . . absolute theological belief

---

* Brotton is particularly interested in the way the treatment of Muslims in English commercial life can be seen to have influenced the treatment of Muslims (and Jews) in English drama. In June of 1596, he explains, "Having coordinated an unlikely alliance involving Muslim Moroccans and Dutch Calvinists, Elizabeth's fleet of 150 ships and 6,000 soldiers left Plymouth . . ." (p. 193). Later in the same year, Shakespeare wrote *The Merchant of Venice*. Brotton suggests that "Shakespeare provides Shylock with a depth of humanity not out of some secret liberal desire to express toleration toward the Jewish faith, but to sharpen the dramatic ambiguity and the power of his character . . ." (p. 197) and that "Shylock is not an attractive character, but Shakespeare deliberately chose to move away from purely villainous stereotypes with the more ambiguous Shylock and Prince of Morocco. The exigencies of politics and trade made alliances with Jews, Turks and Moors necessary . . ." (p. 200). He argues that the influence of Anglo-Islamic trade contributed to the reasons why "Within just over two years of Marlowe's death, Shakespeare had modulated his murderous eastern characters to produce a far more subtle theatre of complicity, where Moors, Jews and Christians—and even the audience—were all equally culpable . . ." (p. 200). He concludes that "Shakespeare grew up under a regime whose isolation from much of Catholic Europe propelled it into alliances with Muslim rulers from Marrakesh, Algiers, Tunis, Constantinople, Qazvin and Isfahan. With the accession of King James, this policy came to an abrupt end, and with it a tradition of representing formidable, eloquent and savage Turks, Moors and Persians on the Elizabethan stage. They would be reinvented in a different key by a new generation of Jacobean playwrights . . ." (p. 297). He notes that the first English chair in Arabic was endowed at Cambridge in 1632, and subsequently one at Oxford in 1636: "England would now try to contain the Islamic world through orientalist scholarship and the painstaking study of philology, archaeology and comparative religion . . ." (p. 298).

often yielded to strategic considerations, political pressures and mercantile interests."[12] If the absolute atheistic convictions of Heydon's elites are to find a rapprochement with religious beliefs, it is unlikely to be because of any commitment to the principle of toleration, but rather because of the specific circumstances of Australian domestic politics and foreign policy. The levels of mutual suspicion, misunderstanding, and ambivalence that attend this rapprochement will also likely be determined by self-interest and any amicable relationship may well entail its own peculiar contradictions.

Heydon also argues that the 'modern elites' have become irrational. Again, he is correct to point out that it is irrational to affirm the right for someone to advocate for a certain position in public discourse, but to deem it as intolerable to oppose that same stance in public discourse. Heydon's critique of the demise of rationality in public life is powerful, and for those of us who remain committed to the disinterested pursuit of knowledge for its own sake, deeply lamentable. When it comes to this demise of rationality, it is again important to remember the significance of practical imperatives. When leaders operate in a polity that does not attach a premium to rationality, it is easy enough for leaders to move into modes of oratory and propaganda that involve influencing audiences by appealing to the audience's emotions, by overwhelming the rational capacity (the sublime), or by sheer intimidation, rather than through persuasion. If Heydon's analysis is accepted, it is telling that whereas reason was once seen as the means by which the tyranny of religious orthodoxy could be overcome, it now seems that rationality might be at risk of being abandoned in the service of suppressing religious minorities.

To the extent that Heydon's elites are intolerant of religious worldviews, it is instructive to consider carefully what he has to say about the religious quest for consolation. He draws out the sense in which the modern world's comforts have rendered incomprehensible the quest for consolation that was more immediately comprehensible in a more inhospitable world.

This is captured in an episode of the Blackadder television series, in which the Prince Regent's butler, Edmund Blackadder, consoles the Prince after some misfortune with the words, "Don't worry, sir, please just consider that life is a valley of woe filled with pain, misery, hunger, and despair." The Prince replies, "Not for me it bloody isn't. As far as I'm concerned, life is a big palace full of food, drink, and comfy sofas."[13] To some extent, most people in a liberal democracy with a welfare state enjoy a life of food, drink, and comfy sofas. The worldviews of religious traditions tend to be formed in a world in which life is more readily characterized by woe, pain, misery, hunger, and despair. The problem of incomprehensibility goes beyond the fact that many people today may not experience the need for consolation that was more apparent in an earlier era. It also goes to the fact that some people who live in a world of comfy sofas maintain that this quest for consolation is still of fundamental importance; and this notwithstanding all the pleasures and comforts that surround them. The religious worldview maintains that there is something important about the quest for consolation that is born of an inhospitable world; and which remains of enduring importance even in a much more physically hospitable world. It is not hard to see how this thought could be incomprehensible to those who do not share it. When, as Heydon suggests, it is political leaders and other 'modern elites' who find such a worldview incomprehensible, this will present significant challenges for their understanding of that part of the population who continue to operate according to such a worldview. To be sure, in a secular state, it might not have been the role of the state to provide consolation. It was understood, at least until recently, that part of the role of state institutions is to create space for non-state institutions to offer consolation. What Heydon warns us is that this becomes increasingly difficult in a world in which the religious quest for consolation becomes incomprehensible to political leaders.

The idea of the "encumbered self" is introduced by the Harvard political theorist, Michael J. Sandel, to argue for a return to understanding religious freedom as a matter of freedom of conscience, not freedom of choice.[14] His use of the concept of the encumbered self might, however, also cast further light on some of Heydon's central contentions. It has already been suggested that we might understand the religious worldview as being incomprehensible to Heydon's elites, and that this poses a fundamental problem for them as democratic leaders. At the core of this incomprehension might be incomprehension of something like Sandel's encumbered self.

Sandel introduces the concept of the encumbered self to make sense of two competing approaches to religious freedom in the Supreme Court of the United States. In some cases, he argues, the court has treated religious freedom as part of a broader freedom to choose one's beliefs. In other cases, the court has treated it as the freedom to obey a duty. Sandel observes that the founding fathers, such as James Madison and Thomas Jefferson, clearly did not conceive of religious freedom as a right to choose one's beliefs. For them, it was undoubtedly a matter of protecting the freedom to perform a religious duty according to the dictates of conscience. As Sandel points out, for Madison and Jefferson, religious liberty is predicated on the idea that beliefs are not a matter of choice.[15] This is at odds with the more recent approach, in which the Supreme Court has upheld religious freedom on the basis that it is a matter of protecting the freedom to choose one's own beliefs.

Sandel distinguishes between beliefs and actions, explaining that beliefs are not governed by will in the way that actions are. A person has no control over his beliefs—we cannot change beliefs that we understand to be true, even if we desire to change them. This becomes important for deciding whether to treat religious freedom as a case of freedom of conscience or freedom of choice. What it means for the law to protect conscience is different from what it means to protect choice, for, as Sandel puts it, "where conscience dictates, choice decides."[16] Whereas Madison and Jefferson would have protected religious freedom as an instance of protecting conscience, or protecting the right to adhere to beliefs that are beyond the control of one's will, the contemporary approach has been to treat it as an instance of protecting choice, or protecting the right to decide what one will do and to act accordingly. This reflects the mission of contemporary political liberalism, which treats religious freedom as a prerequisite for protecting individual autonomy. Sandel's point is that contemporary liberalism means to protect religious freedom, but, in doing so, it fundamentally misunderstands what the religious person needs to protect: "despite its liberating promise, or perhaps because of it, this broader mission deprecates the claim of those for whom religion is not an expression of autonomy but a matter of conviction unrelated to choice."

He introduces the idea of the encumbered self to explain what it means for persons to believe that they are "bound by duties derived from sources other than themselves." Religious freedom, when understood as protection of conscience, is a matter of respecting encumbered selves; when understood as protection of choice, religious freedom is a matter of respecting unencumbered selves. He demonstrates that the different approaches that the Supreme Court has taken can be identified in terms of whether they are approaching religious freedom as a matter of respecting the encumbered self or the unencumbered self, and he believes that this analysis highlights the points of confusion in the case law.[17]

Sandel is ready to admit that although religious freedom is a matter of respecting encumbered selves, not every expression of religiosity involves an encumbered self. Sometimes, religious people do make choices in circumstances in which they do not understand themselves to be obeying a religious duty. For instance, in some circumstances, the erection of a nativity scene in a public place may be an expression of religion, even though there may not be a religious obligation to do this. In such cases, he is prepared to admit that the action is not a matter of conscience, but rather one of choice. The encumbered self is only in need of protection when what is involved is a belief that pervades one's whole way of life, rather than an action that is merely the expression of a personal preference.

Heydon's modern elites are the personification of contemporary liberalism's commitment to freedom of choice. What seems like hostility to religion might, in fact, stem from a failure to comprehend the sense in which the religious worldview is predicated on the idea of the encumbered self; that there are duties that I have in virtue of beliefs about the world that I know to be true, and which I cannot change, however much I—or the elites—might wish I could change them. To those who have a contemporary liberal worldview, personal autonomy is fundamental: on this view, I am the source of all valid claims about what I should and should not do. This worldview will struggle to accommodate the perspective of other persons who believe themselves to be bound by duties that are not derived from themselves. So democratic leaders in a religious world need to find a way to comprehend the worldview of encumbered selves, even if they understand themselves to be unencumbered selves. The failure of democratic leaders to do so results in Heydon's tyranny of relativism.

The idea of the encumbered self is intended to capture more than merely the sense in which religious liberty is a matter of freedom of conscience (rather than freedom of choice of beliefs). Sandel acknowledges that it can also capture the conscientious objector's right to avoid conscription, even if his opposition to war is not anchored in any religious belief. The encumbered self is a richer concept than the duty to adhere to conscience. What it captures is the sense in which there are aspects of my life that are not merely lifestyle choices; they go to my sense of myself, and I cannot but act upon them on pain of ceasing to be myself.

Protecting my fundamental need to adhere to my conscience then becomes an example of the broader sense of protecting my fundamental need to act in a way that does not negate myself, because my conscience is at the core of my understanding of myself. It is worth exploring this idea, because it might also capture concerns that Heydon's modern elites value. In this way, it might help demonstrate that some aspects of the encumbered self that they prize are more intimately related to the duty to adhere to conscience that the encumbered self of the religious worldview prizes.

A good indication that someone's actions genuinely emanate from an encumbered self is the expression of indignation that comes from a response to the claim that the person has simply made a 'lifestyle choice.' We all make lifestyle choices, but sometimes our actions amount to something more than a lifestyle choice. In 2015, the Premier of Western Australia proposed that a number of remote Aboriginal communities needed to be closed down because it was unfeasible for the government to continue to fund them. The prime minister of the day showed his support for the premier, arguing that people in remote communities could not expect the government to continue to fund their lifestyle choices if they were determined to live in extremely remote places.[18]

It is true that it is extremely expensive to provide police, health, education, and a range of other essential services in exceptionally remote places that have very small permanent populations. So, to the extent that the people who live there are making a lifestyle choice, they should be expected to meet the cost of that choice, or else they should accept that they will have to live without the provision of services that would be deemed essential in less remote places. A reasonable person might accept that this is fair and not unduly offensive. The offensiveness comes, however, when an Aboriginal people's connection to country is characterized as a lifestyle choice. The Uluru Statement From the Heart speaks of the ancestral tie between the land and the indigenous peoples "who were born therefrom, remain attached thereto, and must one day return thither to be united with our ancestors." Such a connection to country cannot be characterized as a choice. It is not strictly a case of adhering to conscience, but it is nevertheless a case of another aspect of an encumbered self. What it means for these people to maintain their stewardship of their country might not require them to live in these specific communities. If the government were to work with them to identify other ways in which they could maintain their connection to country; if they could see that they had multiple options for doing so, then it might be a question of lifestyle choice. But the idea that they have some form of connection to their country which they cannot renounce, and that they must live their lives in a way that affirms this connection, is more than a lifestyle choice. It is also something that Heydon's modern elites would readily appreciate to be more than a lifestyle choice. To protect this connection to country is, for his elites, more than simply protecting freedom of choice.

Another context in which indignation is heard very loudly from Heydon's modern elites is when it is suggested that a transgender person makes a lifestyle choice to live as a person of a gender that is not aligned to the reproductive organs with which the person was born. In situations involving sexuality or gender identification, we seem again to be in the domain of the encumbered self. The person in question protests that this is a matter that goes to my fundamental understanding of myself, and not a matter over which there is any genuine choice. Legal protection should be afforded, it will be argued, precisely because it is not a matter of choice. It might not be the case that this is an instance of a person adhering to a duty imposed by conscience. But it does, nevertheless, seem like a case in which some aspect of the encumbered self is in play. As such, we cannot simply fall back on the rhetoric of lifestyle choices. What advocates claim is in need of protection is some aspect of the encumbered self.

A final aspect of the encumbered self might be exposed by a common criticism of utilitarianism as a system of ethics, namely its inability to account for special relationships. The nineteenth-century English utilitarian philosopher and political reformer, J. S. Mill, famously provided a three-stage proof for Jeremy Bentham's theory that we should always act in a way that maximises happiness for the maximum number of people: happiness is desirable in itself; only happiness is desirable in itself; the general happiness is desirable. One common criticism of this argument challenges the idea that everyone's happiness is equally valuable.

Should I really treat my mother's happiness as being as valuable as that of a stranger? We seem to have a strong sense that we should value the people with whom we stand in special relationships more than we value the happiness of total strangers. This may be understood in terms of duties, but even if one were not to formulate it in terms of a duty, it does seem to go to the idea that we are in some way encumbered by these special relationships. Parents do not simply choose to act in their children's best interests. We are inclined to accept that a parent does not believe that there is a choice in these circumstances, and we find it deeply repugnant when confronted with a story of a parent who believed he or she was free to choose to act contrary to the child's best interests. Indeed, this is why the law often demonstrates a tenderness towards the parent, where a child is involved, accepting both that the parent will act in the child's best interests, and that the parent is usually best placed to determine what is in the child's best interest. One way of understanding this might be that the parent's sense of self is encumbered by the special relationship in which he or she stands to the child, such that the parent cannot conceive of himself or herself other than as standing in this relationship. Special relationships, sexuality and gender identification, attachment to country, and religious conscience are, in some sense, very different considerations. If we are able to understand them all as ways in which a self can become encumbered, however, we are able to see that there is something similar about the ethical seriousness of each of these encumbrances on the self.

That ought to have a special significance for Heydon's elites. They may find the idea of an encumbered self incomprehensible, given that they are so preoccupied with the autonomy of unencumbered selves. If they were able to see that some of the concerns that they take very seriously are, in fact, encumbrances on the self that need to be respected, they might find it easier to comprehend the sense in which the dictates of religious conscience that are central to the religious worldview need to be respected as ways in which people are encumbered selves.

Sandel's analysis helps us to understand what it is about religious people as individuals—namely, the sense in which they are encumbered selves—that is incomprehensible to Heydon's elites. There is also a sense, however, in which it is not only religious people who are incomprehensible, but religion as a source of truth. This becomes apparent in the writing of the former Chief Rabbi of the Commonwealth, Lord Sacks of Aldgate, which captures something of the significance of religious belonging in the idea of "the dignity of difference."

In his account of the challenges presented by globalisation, Sacks argues that liberal democracies are ill-equipped to deal with moral challenges precisely because of their strengths: "they have adopted mechanisms that marginalise moral considerations" with the effect that Western politics has "become more procedural and managerial" and increasingly "reluctant to enact a vision of the common good."[19] He is aware that the free market is the institution that has both enabled increasing prosperity and at the same time led to increasing social alienation, but he does not reject the free market as such. Rather, he regards it as an example of "when one institution exceeds its proper bounds and colonises areas that have a different logic and dynamic."[20] He notes that in the past, religion, science, and politics have all exceeded their proper boundaries. Central to his idea of the threat presented by the marketplace is the thought that it has resulted in "covenantal" relationships giving way to "contractual relationships." A covenant, for Sacks, "is a bond, not of interest or advantage, but of belonging" and tends to be made "when two or more people come together to create a 'We'," and, unlike contracts, "tend to be open-ended and enduring."[21] It is in the reciprocity of covenantal relationships that trust is born, and without them, Sacks maintains, there could be no selves or contracts.

It is hardly surprising that a rabbi should extol the virtues of covenant, given that this is at the core of the Jewish religion, which understands its genesis to lie in a covenant between God and Abraham and then a covenant between God and the entire House of Israel at Mount Sinai. What might be surprising, however, are the consequences that he believes flow from the covenant between God and Israel. The obligations of the Torah are obligations that extend only to the Jews. The Jewish conception of monotheism, Sacks explains, never held that the one God offers only one path to salvation. Rather, "it is that *unity is worshipped in diversity*."[22] This leads him to assert that we need not only a theology of commonality but also a theology of difference: "why God asks us to respect the freedom and dignity of those not like us."[23]

As the former Archbishop of Canterbury, Lord Williams of Oystermouth, recently reminded us, tribalism remains a powerful force which we must strive to overcome.[24] Sacks is mindful of this threat: "To surrender the lonely self to something larger, more powerful and elemental, is one of the deepest instincts of mankind."[25] And yet, whilst he acknowledges that we should be on guard against tribalism, he warns that there is also another threat: "The paradox is that the very thing we take to be the antithesis of tribalism—universalism—can also be deeply threatening, and may be equally inadequate as an account of the human situation." It is in response to the challenge of universalism that Sacks proposes the dignity of difference.

The problem of universalism, Sacks argues, is that it suggests "that there is only one truth about the essentials of the human condition, and it holds true for all people at all times."[26] The opening chapters of the Book of Genesis reject this form of universalism according to Sacks. They convey a set of truths through narrative. This is important for Sacks because, in the end, he will argue that moral truths are only compelling when they are conveyed in this way. He rejects the tradition of abstract philosophy that begins with Plato on the basis that "It is *the attempt to impose an artificial unity on divinely created diversity.*"[27] This is the core of his objection to universalism.

Sacks does not subscribe to relativism, however, and he avoids this by proposing a distinction between 'absoluteness' and 'universality'. He argues that the truths of the Bible are *absolutely* true, but that they are *particular* rather than universal. This is why they can only be posited through a particular narrative. The bonds of parenthood and love are given as examples of the particular absolute. The parent feels a bond to this particular child, not to children indiscriminately; the lover feels affection for a particular person in all his uniqueness, not merely as an instance of a generalised affection for a type. Sacks argues that it is the absolute particular that we should be affirming in politics. He finds a theological basis for this in the idea that we should see God's image in anyone who happens not to be in our own image. This leads to an obligation to take difference seriously. Tolerance alone is not enough to take difference seriously. Greece, Rome, and the Enlightenment all represented universalist cultures that, Sacks argues, prided themselves on their tolerance, but, like contemporary forms of tolerance, such as political correctness, their tolerance "turned out to be highly circumscribed."[28]

Sacks does not hold out much hope that the human rights discourse of the post-Second World War era will uphold the dignity of difference because it too succumbs to universalism: "It suggests that the particularities of a culture are mere accretions to our essential and indivisible humanity, instead of being the very substance of how most people learn what it is to be human."[29] He recruits the Oxford political theorist, Sir Isaiah Berlin, to his cause, quoting Berlin's critique of individuals and groups who believe that they are in the sole possession of the truth. Such people, Berlin and Sacks believe, cannot but maintain that anyone who disagrees with them cannot be right. In Berlin's words, "This makes one certain that there is *one* goal and only one for one's nation or church or the whole of humanity, and that it is worth any amount of suffering (particularly on the part of other people) if only the goal is attained . . ."[30]

This thought has special relevance for Heydon's elites. They assume that Australian society has one goal, and that religion needs to be eliminated in pursuit of that goal, whatever suffering this might cause to some people. They fail to appreciate that some people in Australia might identify different goals, and that respect for the place of religion in some people's lives might be important in order to allow them to pursue their goals.

Sacks is not keen on the seventeenth-century conception of the 'individual' as an entity which has a stable sense of self from birth to death, and which is the basic unit of society. It is this individual that is capable of having 'identity' and which then forms the basis of contemporary identity politics. Rather, he believes that we need to understand ourselves as part of communities of meaning. Yes, the members of these communities have absolute value, because each is made in the image of God, but their absolute truths can only be articulated through the particular communities to which they belong. Hence the truth articulated by these communities is absolute but also particular. This is an attempt to renounce universalism without embracing relativism.

This is also why Sacks believes religions have a special role within society; a role that cannot be performed by an abstract system of philosophy. Unlike philosophical systems, which can also offer a vision of the good through abstract reasoning, religions embody their vision of the good "in the life of a community."[31] For Sacks, the awareness that absolute meaning comes through belonging to a particular community naturally creates room for the dignity of difference. Once I understand that my absolute meaning is derived from belonging to my particular community, my commitment to the dignity of the other—who is created in the image of God—requires me to respect his absolute truth, which emanates from the particular community to which he belongs. Again, this is a challenge for Heydon's elites. Their commitment to relativism means that they cannot comprehend the thought that the absolute meaning of some of their compatriots' lives might be derived from their sense of belonging, rather than from their identity as individuals, which is the basis of the meaning of the lives of Heydon's modern elites.

Sacks cites Francis Fukuyama on the inadequacy of relativism, which "must ultimately end up undermining democratic and tolerant values . . . Relativism is not a weapon that can be aimed selectively at the enemies one chooses . . . If nothing can be true absolutely, if all values are culturally determined, then cherished principles like human equality have to go by the wayside as well."[32] In a globalised world, Sacks argues that the dignity of difference is the kind of principle that we require to navigate our way in a pluralist world: "fundamentalism, like imperialism, is the attempt to impose a single way of life on a plural world," whereas the dignity of difference is about making space for difference:

> This is not the cosmopolitanism of those who belong nowhere, but the deep human understanding that passes between people who, knowing how important their attachments are to them, understand how deeply someone else's different attachments matter to them also.[33]

According to the dignity of difference, salvation lies in the principles of a particular way of life, not in abstract morality. It admits that "the paths to salvation are many"[34] but they are collective—it is through belonging that we acquire ultimate meaning in our lives, not through the individual act of 'identifying'.

He has no more confidence in toleration than he does in relativism, which he claims essentially "privatised conscience."[35] Yes, toleration allows people to live according to the dictates of their own private consciences—their encumbered selves—but it is inadequate when the strong central power of the state has been decentralised through globalisation. This is because globalisation involves "decentralisation of power combined with maximum vulnerability such that individual acts of terror can destabilise large parts of the world while remaining beyond the reach of any one state, even a superpower . . ."[36]

Heydon's warning about the tolerance of the modern elites seems to be at home in Sacks's thinking. They need to acknowledge that their form of universal truth must give way to a form of pluralism that restricts the power of religions in civil society, whilst at the same time acknowledging their function as sources of absolute particular meaning: "As systems of meaning and purpose, the great world faiths have never been surpassed. As a substitute for politics, however, they are full of danger—and that, in some parts of the world, is what they have become."[37]

It might seem that Heydon's elites are the standard-bearers of the dignity of difference. In a sense this is true—but not in Sacks's sense. They are committed to difference based on identity rather than difference based on belonging. So they are keen to affirm the importance of individual difference, rather than collective difference. This is a fundamental problem from Sacks's perspective, because it is collective difference, or belonging, that makes a special contribution to ethical life that cannot be replicated by individual difference. Alas, the ethical significance of belonging—the dignity of difference—is incomprehensible to Heydon's elites.

Sacks understands that in the contemporary secularised market-driven and globalised world, "The wisdom of the world's religions may seem at best irrelevant, at worst dangerous"; it is perceived to be either too powerless or too powerful, and either way is "part of the problem rather than part of the solution."[38] Sacks maintains, however, that religion needs to be seen as part of the solution because it speaks to concerns to which the institutions of liberal democracy do not speak. The institutions through which we maintain democratic power are fundamentally procedural. These institutions, like the institutions of market capitalism, cannot address problems that involve value. One response is to say that all questions involving value should be left to the individual, but Sacks will argue that propositions about fundamental value can only be embodied in the narratives and institutions of community.

So he is committed to the idea that religions "embody truths unavailable to economics and politics."[39]

As Australian society becomes increasingly less religious, it should not come as a surprise that religion is increasingly incomprehensible to democratic leaders drawn from that less religious society. If there are practical imperatives for engaging seriously both with the religious minority of the Australian population and the increasingly religious international population, democratic leaders will find the motivation to overcome this incomprehension. This also requires vigilance to avert the risk that incomprehension of religion gives way to outright hostility towards it. That religious conscience gives rise to an encumbered self should not be incomprehensible to leaders if they reflect on other senses of the encumbered self that are more immediately comprehensible to them. That religious belonging might be a social asset, rather than a social liability, is something non-religious leaders should reflect on when thinking about how to manage difference in society.

RESPONDING TO BRYAN TURNER AND DAMIEN FREEMAN

1

Amen to Holy Land in Australia

Luke Gosling

ESIDES SPORTS, few things raise blood pressure quite like religion and politics. But they have more noble things in common than the passions they can arouse in us: the glorious heights they have both attained in the history of humanity, as well as the sombre chapters both have known. They meet in the ethical question of what we ought to do to live the good life. Surprisingly, they also share a core concept of faith: the one in man, the other in the divine. This point may seem out of place but there is no doubt that modern political life owes much of its grip on the human mind and heart to the religious traditions that shaped it.

There are many ways in which politics and religion are intimately related, and I don't mean in cases of religiously motivated political leaders or movements. They're both impacted by the advancing secularisation of the public sphere, driven by the decline over recent decades in people's identification with the Christian beliefs and values that have underpinned Western societies, legal systems, and ethical codes for centuries. This creeping de-Christianisation of public life superficially seems to make it less religious and, according to a worldview which welcomes this, more rational and, therefore, better. But this isn't true.

Some worry about what it will mean when public discourse no longer even pretends to be about competing visions of the ideal state and the public good. One alternative is to adopt the American Civil War-era historian Henry Adams's cynical view that politics boils down to "the systematic organization of hatreds." Is this what politics is, in the absence of a widely shared worldview and values to order and elevate public life? That's certainly not what I signed up for.

Much has been written about the post-Christian left, meaning the rise of progressive political causes overtly hostile to Christian values, which was unthinkable in the West until quite recently. In jest, I'm tempted to correct the record by pointing out the Bible's well-known left-wing bias: camels and needles, Jesus' radical humanity and all that. But this isn't the issue. The real issue is cultural and cuts across politics. The foreign editor at *The Australian* newspaper, Greg Sheridan, makes a similar point in his recent book, *God is Good for You: A Defence of Christianity in Troubled Times*. Sheridan quotes the *New York Times* columnist, Ross Douthat, who warned: "If you don't like the religious right, wait till you meet the post-religious right."

There is a risk that post-religious public life will become increasingly less civil, as Turner notes. It risks devolving into Lenin's famous formula for politics: "who beats whom?" It's true that politics, when divorced from the public good and the quest for the good life, is just a naked struggle for power and its exercise. The rising hyper-partisanship, excessive tribalism and demonization of anyone who thinks differently to us, which we are increasingly seeing in Australia and across the West, is not a sign of progress in my view. We're actually regressing towards a politics of 'might makes right', one in which a violent knock on the door is the final argument

We have seen this before. The blood-soaked twentieth century elevated this kind of politics to an art form. Every politics student learns about the horseshoe theory of political ideology. It contains a simple but profound truth: at the extremes, ideological differences become a parody because all extremists resemble one another by their fanaticism and willingness to crush others. Fascism and communism, both of which supposedly opposed each other at the level of ideas, were in practice first cousins and proponents of a hate-based politics. Each led to death camps. We often forget that the name of Hitler's party had 'socialist' and 'workers' in it. My point is not about Nazism: it's that *all* forms of political extremism tend to end in mass graves.

As Sheridan argues, the resurgence of extremism we're seeing across the spectrum and especially in the West is occurring in a God-shaped void in our culture. "The lack of purpose and meaning, the lack of any ultimate standards that come with the exile of God from our culture lead to savage polarisations and sudden outbursts of hysterical sentiments," as he writes. I would only add that the extremist political views that are now thriving in the West, basically all of which reject Christian ideas around stable and unchanging moral standards, tend to be *intolerantly* moralistic in attributing absolute good and absolute evil to their allies and enemies.

Worryingly, this religiously inspired moralism lacks the humbling awareness of the splinter in our own eyes, of our fallenness and of the need for forgiveness and repentance. In short, modern extremists reject God but keep a theology, which they warp to suit their political agendas. What you end up with is the intoxicating idea that man is the one true god, judge, and executioner. The two major twentieth century ideologies were mutated theologies which both worshipped demi-gods. It is strange to think of it this way, but both were violent cults with Man at their apex. Whereas the Bolsheviks were explicitly atheistic, the Nazis were more covert. But had they won the war, they had ambitious plans to de-Christianise Germany and replace the Bible with *Mein Kampf.*

This is important to remember, because many critics who deny religious thought and values any place in public life often defend pseudo-religious worldviews, whether they know it or not. Everyone has or needs a worldview to function in the world, however flimsy. There are of course better and worse worldviews. But a problem arises when groups take theirs to be the 'natural' worldview which is beyond all critique. That's when you get dogmatism. If I assume that how I see the world is the only correct or natural way, and you disagree with me and pick holes in my worldview, I'm more likely to treat you with contempt. The opposite stance—seeing our shared frailty in this business—leads not to relativism but to compassion.

To give a concrete example, the popular belief that Science will redeem humanity by stamping out error, ignorance, and 'obscurantism' is a popular trope hammered by modern atheists who portray science as the one and only highroad to a morally better world. It's an old idea but it has resurfaced in the last century with particular force and fervour. What ends up happening, if you follow the thread of articles of faith like 'God is dead, science proves it', is that you see an entire competing worldview emerge that actively tries to obliterate another.

In her book, *Evolution as Religion*, the British and explicitly non-religious philosopher Mary Midgley quotes the biochemist Jacque Monod as the proponent of one such science-centric worldview that explicitly seeks to lay low every competitor in one fell swoop. He writes: "It is perfectly true that science attacks values" and "subverts" the "animist tradition", under which he lists Aboriginal spirituality, Marxism, and implicitly Christianity. Now for the good news:

> If he accepts this message in its full significance, man must at last wake out of his millenary dream and discover his total solitude, his fundamental isolation. He must realise that . . . he lives on the boundary of an alien world; a world that is deaf to his music, and as indifferent to his hopes as it is to his sufferings or his crimes.

Of course, science says no such thing at all. It doesn't speak with one voice and it can't give us our values and worldviews. Midgley points out that the above is pure 'myth', by which she doesn't mean it's necessarily wrong, but that it's made of the same stuff as a religious worldview. We may *choose* to believe the universe is deaf to our music and indifferent to our sufferings, if we like. But this is a leap of faith, since no scientific data can or ever will confirm it. Religion, for believers, is true myth: traditional stories explaining natural, supernatural, or moral truths that can be comfortably held alongside a deep respect for the scientific method.

It's tempting to mock or vilify views different from ours, but that's precisely what we must not do. The proper response to encountering a worldview so different from our own is at least to treat *the person* with respect, even if we find their views abhorrent. That's what civility means in public life: to love even your adversaries. The growing incivility we're seeing means just the opposite: denigrating, belittling, and mocking another's views or opinions seamlessly turns into a kangaroo court lynching of that person's character, motives, and morals, with no recourse or presumption of innocence. We should sadly expect more of this behaviour as the Christian values that used to form a solid bridge across Australian politics erode and are themselves vilified.

Some think this is a good thing and that we are capable of inventing new secular values and morals to order our society without a notion of the transcendent. The difficulty of achieving this becomes obvious when you consider the rise of what Turner calls "DIY hybrid religiosity", which is associated with the growing 'spiritual but not religious' category in censuses. Rather than becoming more rational and scientifically oriented, as some had hoped and argued, post-Christian Western societies are actually becoming more 'religious' in a much looser sense. Everything from shamanism to witchcraft and occult pagan religions are enjoying revivals today. But there is an even more serious challenge to rebuilding civility and unity in public life.

At the same time as they abandon organized religion, many in the West are turning to what could be called 'personal' religions and directing their worship to various aspects of their own lives. What I mean by this is that many people are taking an increasingly 'religious' attitude towards their chosen object as sacred and worthy of worship: be it what they eat, the environment, their retweets, their Instagram photos, their body, sports, music, or money. Increasingly often, the supreme object of worship is not a personal God or another supernatural mystery, but what one cares about most or one's own self, which are sometimes one and the same thing.

In line with this trend, many people today consider morality to be a private matter. We can each have a personal morality in which *we* decide what is right and wrong. The handy thing is that, since we are the maker and the judge of our own values, we can really decide if we feel like living by them on any particular day. And if we do feel like it, we can also change our values. And if our atomised morality crashes into another person's, we can always invent a new one. What could possibly go wrong? We should care to the extent that this fracturing of people into their separate little curated and individualised moral worlds will have socio-political impacts.

Well, each to their own, we might say. You do you. I do me. We'll interact when we want something from each other, and we'll call that a 'society'. The problem with this approach, we're learning, is that it undermines mutual good-faith, compromise, and consensus-building. Twitter or Facebook-lynchings are just a symptom of this tendency to no longer see *all* human beings as sacred reflections of the divine, leading to a dangerous dehumanisation on all sides. When we convince ourselves that other people are evil villains acting in bad faith because they don't share our views, not only are we very far from the divine, we're far from the idea of the innate dignity of all people found in most religious traditions to varying extents.

This goes to the question of what a person of faith ought to do in public life. In a Western democracy, religiously inspired politicians, and especially Christians, have as their essential task not to preach their creed but to model their values with their deeds. Their task is to honour their values of service, forgiveness, and self-sacrifice by always being predisposed to see error in their own eye before seeing it in others' eyes; to admit when they are wrong; to treat the last as the first; and to strive to unite people, heal divisions, and uphold the dignity of every human being— even their rivals and especially them. No politician, no person can reach such moral heights alone, but perfection is the standard we need to aim for.

In his essay, Freeman writes about liberal democracies being increasingly reluctant to offer a vision of the common good, preferring a managerial approach to the riskier one of giving people a shared sense of belonging that goes beyond cheesy clichés like 'we're all in this together'. This will have civilisational implications. If citizens are reduced to the status of customers in a Westfield shopping centre, with the state only existing to provide administration, marketing, cleaning staff, and car park security, and when all advertisements tell each shopper the whole experience is about *them*, can we really be surprised to see toilet paper hoarding or food riots the day there is want or crisis on our shores? This, I think, is what the Christian apologist C. S. Lewis had in mind when he said we make people "without chests and expect of them virtue and enterprise. We laugh at honour and are shocked to find traitors in our midst."[1]

Though Australia is an increasingly a-religious nation, I have every confidence that the majority of Australians are bound by the ethos of mateship, duty, and sacrifice that permeates our national identity and worldview. The Australian War Memorial is a truly sacred institution in our nation. I mention this because it, too, is built on the same bedrock commitment to universal values that transcend our particular interests and can demand great self-sacrifice. It, too, will be increasingly under challenge for the same reasons.

To stay strong and free; to enjoy our liberty, this worldview must be defended, if we're to be bound by more than polite nods in the carpark. Rights have always come paired with responsibilities. The military ethos of self-sacrifice reminds us of their essential connection. In her moving poem about the late Corporal Cameron Baird VC MG, Corporal E Rowland concluded:

> This was the plan, God had all along,
> to teach us how we should live.
> Living your life as a sacrifice,
> not to take but how we should give.
> So rest in peace young Burnie Boy,
> your legacy will remain.
> For the debt you paid, we'll never forget,
> for it fuels the eternal flame.

If duty ever becomes a joke and faith is declared anathema on our shores, we will no longer be living in Australia and we will no longer be a democracy. We see again how closely the fates of faith and politics are actually linked. We may not want a faith-based politics, but a faith-*informed* politics is in the common good. The cornerstones of our democracy are universal principles like freedom, fairness, justice, the rule of law. But in today's politics, universalism is increasingly dissolving into the demands of particular individuals or groups.

What people of all faiths bring to political life, whether they practice Islam, Jainism, Sikhism, Hinduism, Judaism, Buddhism, Christianity, or an Aboriginal belief system, is a commitment to values that transcend our individual wants and needs. If we have leaders who help others to see the constructive intuitions in these traditions—including in the Indigenous connection with land, sea, sky, and all creatures great and small—then we've got a chance of upholding the holiness of life, the dignity of every person, and of living more sustainably on this planet.

The spiritual dimension of the fight against climate change was made clear when Pope Francis described the destruction of the environment as a sin, which, in the Catholic tradition, means a direct affront to God's law. Muslim leaders made similar points in the Islamic Declaration on Climate Change, as did the Dalai Lama when he rightly called it "very illogical" simply to pray to God or Buddha to fix our own ecological mess; to absolve us of moral responsibility for sins for which we're still unrepentant.

Religious traditions remind all of us engaged in public life that sending 'thoughts and prayers' can be a virtue-signalling way to justify not acting on our moral obligations. That's why rebuilding the ethical infrastructure of our communities and our nation is very much in the public interest as it will strengthen our social resilience, our national security, and our international reputation. "In terms of international standards of citizenship and human rights," as Turner rightly points out, the "treatment of Aboriginal peoples raises ongoing questions about Australia's ranking in human rights terms." When I spoke in Parliament on reconciliation recently, I talked about the "message of the carpenter, Jesus Christ". I sent the speech to my dad. He reminded me that the words of the carpenter are good but dead if not put into action by those with the power to make change a reality.

Our nation will not be a great one until we are able to tell the truth about settlement, forgive each other our trespasses, see our service to each other to the benefit of all, and to see our self-sacrifice as strengthening the common good. Peter Steele, the Jesuit priest and poet, once reflected on the state of Australian society thus: "Australia does not need to exist in a state of sterility; the desert does not need to be our story. Do pray, talk and plan, so that we may become what we were always meant to be—a Holy Land." Amen to that and to the building of a general Australian consensus akin to how the First Australians exercise 'caring for country'.

I love the Light on the Hill speech by the sixteenth prime minister of Australia, Ben Chifley, which was inspired by the Salt and Light section of Jesus' Sermon on the Mount in Matthew's Gospel.* Chifley's speech exhorted the true believers to work "for the betterment of mankind, not only here but anywhere we may give a helping hand. If it were not for that, the Labor movement would not be worth fighting for." The News Limited journalist, Adam Creighton, recently wrote that "the light on the hill has recently become a disco ball in a gay nightclub, with race-

---

* Ye are the salt of the earth: but if the salt have lost his savour, wherewith shall it be salted? it is thenceforth good for nothing, but to be cast out and trodden under foot of men. Ye are the light of the world. A city set on a hill cannot be hid. Neither do [men] light a lamp, and put it under the bushel, but on the stand; and it shineth unto all that are in the house. Even so let your light shine before men; that they may see your good works, and glorify your Father who is in heaven." (Matthew 5:13-16).

based entry caps."[2] Of course, I appreciate the freedom he has to express that opinion whilst I reflect on what Jesus preached: "Thou shalt love thy neighbour as thyself" (also Matthew).

Loving my neighbour as myself is something I try to do every day in political life. It's hard when the vicious hyper-politicisation of the public arena rewards uncharitable behaviour. But that is what I strive for because the values I represent are those of Labor's social justice mission foretold by Chifley and those that my parents, my religious tradition, my military service, and my mentors have endowed me with over the course of my life. My mission and my calling in this season of life are to fulfil my duty in the democratic process to the best of my abilities and to honour the mandate entrusted to me by Australians. I am grateful to the traditions I was raised in, religious and military, which keep my eyes on the public good.

Freeman has eloquently warned that "as Australian society becomes increasingly less religious, it should not come as a surprise that religion is increasingly incomprehensible to democratic leaders drawn from that less religious society." This is true and concerning.

Whether we are people of religious faith, or people who draw their meaning from science, or art, or family, all of us who strive to be people of goodwill must do our bit to expand the narrowing circle of compassion, comprehension, justice, love, and forgiveness.

Whatever our creed or beliefs or opinions, we must speak truth to power, whether that's in the geostrategic realm, within the Australian polity, or in our local communities, so that we honour and cultivate the holiness of our land and bequeath to our children a better and more harmonious world. These essays help us to recognise that urgent civic and sacred duty.

2

Accommodating religious diversity in Australian democracy

Dean Smith

WHILE AUSTRALIA is commonly characterized as a secular country and the 1900 Constitution of the Commonwealth of Australia prohibits the Commonwealth Government from establishing a church "or prohibiting the free exercise of any religion",[1] the consideration and influence of religious matters has often been at the heart of Australia's cultural and democratic development. So it should come as no surprise that Australians can have a high degree of confidence that Australia's democratic structures will provide for a very satisfactory accommodation of the challenge of increasing religious diversity.

It has been said that Australia's early settlers were more likely to attend a Christian church than a pub, with colonial settlements often erecting a place of worship before they built their local public house. Indeed, many convicts embraced the Christian church along their path to moral reformation and redemption. Throughout Australia's history, the role of Christian denominations in the development of education, health, and welfare services has always been encouraged, and despite the existence of secular government, these institutions have often been generously financed by Australian taxpayers. In return, this largesse has built a network of not-for-profit and faith-based charities that are unaligned to the state, but which the community trusts to be effective and efficient providers of essential care services for the aged, disabled, and homeless, as well as early childhood, primary, secondary, and tertiary education.

Australia's democratic discourse has regularly been punctuated by contentious debates that, while not of a wholly religious character, were led by individuals influenced by their religious perspective and loyalties—the 1916 and 1917 referenda on conscription, 'the Split' inside the political wing of Australia's trade union movement in the 1950s, and the long debate about how to afford legal equality for same-sex couples. These seminal debates are now synonymous with names like the Most Reverend Henry Lowther Clarke (Anglican Archbishop of Melbourne), the Most Reverend Daniel Mannix (Roman Catholic Archbishop of Melbourne), Mr B. A. Santamaria, the Honourable Tony Abbott AC, and the Most Reverend Anthony Fisher OP (Roman Catholic Archbishop of Sydney).

Australia has seen many strong political leaders with clear religious loyalties and motivations, but, until relatively recently, there was a strong correlation between Christian religious observance and political party affiliation. It has been argued that Protestants historically gravitated to conservative parties, where they advocated for causes linked to moral improvement, including strong opposition to gambling and promotion of temperance, while Roman Catholics organized themselves in the labour movement as a bulwark against the growing appeal of socialism.[2] Even in this new millennium, around a quarter of Christians are said to attend church weekly, the same proportion of all school students attend church-affiliated schools, and the Christian religious festivals of Easter and Christmas are extended public holidays. The most recent census identified that 52.1% of Australians classified themselves as Christian, almost 23% identified themselves as Catholic and just over 13% as Anglican. These major Christian denominations also witnessed the greatest fall in observance—decreasing from 63.9% to 52.1%. And yet, Australia's changing demographics and religious diversity are becoming more distinguishable, leading to the accurate characterization of Australia as a pluralistic religious nation.

Australia has probably always been slightly more religiously pluralist than we are in the habit of acknowledging. The First Fleet is believed to have carried at least fifteen Jews, and convicts were often transported to Australia for their religiously motivated political views. Today, almost 10% of Australians identified themselves as followers of non-Christian religions, including Muslims (2.6%), Buddhists (2.4%), Hindus (1.9%), Sikhs (0.5%), and Jews (0.4%). And it is the rate of growth of these non-Christian religious communities that will present the most interesting, and important, future narrative about religion and democracy in Australia. Over the last decade, the fastest growing religious classifications have been 'No Religion'—up from 18.7% to 30.1%, Hinduism—up from 0.7% to 1.9%, Islam—up from 1.7% to 2.6%, and Sikhism—up from 0.1% to 0.5%. In fact, it is now established that Hinduism is the fastest growing religion in absolute numbers in every State and Territory of Australia. This observation challenges where the emphasis should be placed in the debate over religious freedom in Australia.

This debate is often framed as either one in which traditional Christian denominations are being challenged by new, youthful evangelical denominations, or instead as one which regards all Christian denominations as under threat by a 'foreign' religion, where suspicions may be exacerbated by broader and international political considerations. When the religious freedom debate is viewed, however, through an alternate lens of the *fastest* growing religions in Australia, that is those of non-Abrahamic traditions, we may find less tension between religion and democracy than we first expected.

In this discussion it can be tempting to assess our modern political, cultural, and religious contest as one of 'erosion and crisis'. But an equally defensible characterization could be 'evolution and accommodation'. Thus, when Turner presents us with the question, "Is religion part of the problem or part of the solution of democracy?" he invites us into too narrow a discussion. By accepting the narrow and binary approach, we fail to acknowledge properly the evolutionary path that has led to Australia accommodating an ever-widening range of faiths and being regarded as an open, tolerant, and respectful nation for all. It would be incorrect to assume that the conflict between religion and democracy in Australia will reflect the same trajectory predicted for the United Kingdom, Europe, and the United States. Turner is right to identify the corrosive influence of populism, political extremism, and the dismantling of globalism as a "daunting crisis for democracies", however, a more complete analysis would acknowledge the positive influence of certain structural features of liberal democracies on tempering and taming some of these crises.

When Freeman describes the challenges for democratic leaders as struggling to comprehend the "significance of religion", he overlooks the real possibility that this incomprehension of religious attitudes could be as alive between religious people as it is between religious and non-religious people. This becomes particularly acute in the Australian context when we consider the ability and willingness of people to comprehend the religious views of people of faiths other than Christianity.

The presence of two specific characteristics that are unique to Australia's democratic structure—compulsory voting and bicameralism—have the power to deliver a more constructive and civil resolution to the religion and democracy debate. In Australia, these characteristics were originally designed to ensure a widened franchise delivered a popularly endorsed mandate and to reconcile the rights of Australia's smaller colonies with the wealth and population of Victoria and New South Wales. Almost one hundred and twenty years later, their modern role has been to act as a powerful but invisible moderating influence over the "daunting crisis" of the populism and extremism identified by Turner. They are also illuminating when we seek a deeper appreciation of Australia's success in accommodating the tensions between religion and democracy. This occurs at a time when contemporaries in the United Kingdom and United States are experiencing difficulty and conflict when trying to balance democratic virtues with greater religious liberties and protections.

The well-established and accepted practice of compulsory voting, accompanied by variations of preferential voting across Australia, is relatively rare. Australia is one of just thirty-two nations with compulsory voting, and one of only nineteen that enforces compliance through a financial penalty. Compulsory voting has been a hallmark of Australian democratic practice since it was first introduced in Queensland in 1915 and has been described as "one of those unique local practices which contributes so much to the fairness of Australian elections".[3]

Although compulsory voting was first advocated by Alfred Deakin at the turn of the twentieth century, it was not introduced at the federal level until the passage of a private member's bill in 1924. The impact was immediate, with election turnout rising to over 91%. At the previous election, turnout had been just 58.7% and averaged 63.5% over the nine federal elections since Federation. Victoria introduced compulsory voting in 1926, New South Wales and Tasmania in 1928, Western Australia in 1936, and South Australia in 1942. Its broad acceptance is demonstrated by voter turnout never having fallen below 90%.

It is significant that Australian is the only English-speaking nation in the world to compel its citizens to vote. And yet, although its impact on civic debate and lawmaking is critical, it is all too often overlooked. The existence and impact of compulsory voting on the body politic is profound, not least in isolating extreme views, and driving the political discourse to the middle-ground. It moderates the public discussion between politicians and voters, the debates within political parties, and the lobbying of those seeking to influence legislators, because electoral success is secured by winning the centre, not from mobilising the extremes.

For matters of a religious character, the moderating influence of compulsory voting has the effect of allowing religious perspectives and attitudes with the broadest common appeal to be incorporated into the political, while those beliefs of a more contested character may exist at the periphery of the public discourse.

This 'pursuit of the centre' dynamic is further assisted by the preferential voting system, which, in effect, requires the elector to choose the 'least-worst-alternative' candidate or policy from the field. It combines to provide a broader legitimacy and mandate to a successful candidate, political party, or policy position being contested. It is the absence of this feature in the United Kingdom and the United States that permits their electoral systems to be more easily dominated by single-issue politics.

The existence of bicameral parliaments is key to Australia's constitution. Bicameralism is the term given to representative decision-making which requires legislation to be contested and passed by two different chambers—at the federal level in Australia, these are the House of Representatives and the Senate. Its virtues include quality control over the lawmaking, a safeguard against the misuse of power by executive government and/or a unicameral assembly, and prevention of the "control of one body by a political faction not properly representative of the whole community".[4] On a practical level, bicameralism has improved the quality of parliaments, ensured the proper consideration of views and issues across geographically, culturally, and religiously diverse communities, and allows parliaments to be truly representative of the people that elect them.

The essays promoting the design of the American Constitution, known as *The Federalist Papers*, noted that an inherent weakness and danger of unicameral assemblies was "the propensity of all single and numerous assemblies . . . to yield to the impulse of sudden and violent passions, and to be seduced by factious leaders, into intemperate and pernicious resolutions".[5] In Australia, bicameralism at the federal level and in all State parliaments (except Queensland) is a "product of constitutional intent and design, not of evolutionary process"[6] and has proven itself a subtle but significant feature in ensuring Australia's political system can accommodate changing political and societal trends.

Our bicameral experience has been further enhanced by the decision to ensure each of the two legislative chambers are constituted by different electoral methods. This has greatly moderated against the excesses of power that could be exercised by the majority while these structural limitations on power increase accountability, and limit a government's ability to act with disregard for those not represented by the majority. But,

critically, the broad use of proportional representation as one of two electoral methods ensures the widest possible range of views are accommodated in proportion to their electoral support.

In recent times obvious beneficiaries of this have been political voices with a strong religious tone including former Democratic Labor Party Senator John Madigan, Family First Senators Bob Day and Lucy Gichuhi, and Fred Nile's Call to Australia Party. So, when it comes to considering the place of religious life and attitudes in our public discourse, the response should not be one of fear for the future, but quiet confidence based on our past experience. In the Australian context, there is recent evidence to suggest that tensions can result in an acceptable resolution, even harmony.

In December 2017, the Australian Parliament legislated for same-sex couples to be given the same legal recognition as heterosexual couples under the Marriage Act. The Bill was the twenty-third legislative attempt, but the first to include religious exemptions which allowed religious institutions to continue to observe their doctrinal attitudes regarding marriage, free from legal prosecution. Put to a popular vote through a plebiscite, the proposition received majority support in every State and Territory in Australia. When the matter was later debated in the Parliament, debate concentrated not on whether there should be an accommodation of religious views, but the form and scope of protections for such views. The measure of how appropriate the final accommodation of religious protections was is best demonstrated by the fact that, since the matter was resolved by the Parliament in late 2017, there has been very little if any controversy surrounding the final balance struck between religious observance and the improvement in the legal standing of same-sex couples.

There is great solace in the clear evidence that Australia's democratic structures, and their track record in moderating the excesses of political or religious influence, are something in which we can continue to place our trust. More particularly, it is not necessary for those in public life to look to the emerging experiences in other countries for guidance on how specific issues will play out here in Australia. It is the uniqueness of the structural features of Australian democracy that make us very well placed to navigate the expected tensions between religion and democracy.

3

Leadership and society in a less monochromatic world

Ursula Stephens

B RYAN TURNER AND DAMIEN FREEMAN have crafted two contemporary and contemplative essays to examine how liberal societies and their leadership are both intertwined with, and challenged by, the changing nature of religious beliefs and practices. Although framed on the cusp of the Covid-19 pandemic that has swept the world, the essays explore longstanding issues to juxtapose two contested positions about the influence of religion on leadership and society and offer insights into how these positions will continue to change.

I have now read these essays several times during the Covid-19 lockdown and each time I am reminded of the importance of connection, community, and the need to make sense of the incomprehensible. Much has been written in recent months on the mental health impacts of imposed social isolation, and more has been written about the benefits that Covid-19 has brought to our world including a deeper sense of connection and spiritual wellbeing. When so much of our everyday lives has been changed, there are many who are searching for greater meaning in the spiritual and religious dimensions of our lives.

It was the English lawyer, Christopher McCrudden, who described five common dimensions of the three key religious traditions: Judaism, Christianity, and Islam. First, each religion specifies a set of *beliefs* which are of transcendent importance to believers. Second, each promotes a set of *values*. Third, these values are manifested by *practice*, both public and private. Fourth, each religion has some *institutional structure* which authorises particular individuals to maintain orthodoxy and orthopraxis— right thinking and right action. Fifth, each of these religions provides the followers with a *social status* or *social identity*. Beliefs, values, practice, institutional structure, and social identity can all help an individual maintain a sense of connectedness and wholeness amidst the mess and complexity of daily life.[1]

While witnessing the bushfire devastation of the 2019-20 summer, many people of faith found themselves saying, "There was nothing I could do but pray." Those without faith might think they could have done more, or that prayer could achieve nothing, but at least through prayer, the religious person in that moment of powerlessness is thrown back into that comprehensive world of relationships—with God, with humanity, and with the whole of creation.

As a member of the Australian Senate, I joined the Parliamentary Christian Fellowship and for a period was its chairperson, which provided me with insights into the motivations of some of the most controversial and confrontational politicians in our national Parliament.

Each Tuesday morning, we left our political allegiances at the door and met in fellowship to discuss the challenges, ethics, and concerns about issues that were currently under consideration within the Parliament. There was never a sense that confidences shared in that room would be betrayed, or referred to outside the group—there was always a sense that here, in this place, at this time, the ethical and moral foundations of our shared Christianity informed our prayers and discussions, and, I certainly believe, helped to influence policymaking and voting patterns in the Parliament.

So, in my current role as CEO of Catholic Social Services Australia, I have had many reasons to reflect on the work and influence of the Parliamentary Christian Fellowship. Known best for organising the National Prayer Breakfast, the ecumenical service for the beginning of each parliamentary year, and sponsoring the parliamentary chaplain, the Parliamentary Christian Fellowship has provided a spiritual space for many parliamentarians over many decades.

There is no designated space in the Parliament House for those meetings. It was Bob Hawke, who, as prime minister, rejected the notion that there be a chapel included in the design. There is, however, a space called the Meditation Room, and it is here that our group met each sitting fortnight to share concerns about constituents, to offer prayers in support of colleagues in distress, and to pray for wisdom and justice in the work of the Parliament. Few people would know how important and effective that group was in negotiating within and across party lines on issues of conscience and social justice, amendments to legislation, and public statements in times of crisis.

This is why I have enjoyed reading these essays so much. Turner takes us through the challenges to institutional religion posed by the increasingly secular character of modern societies. He cites numerous examples of public policy issues that were subject to furious public and private advocacy, using all the traditional levers of influence, as well as new forms of advocacy and influence that have emerged through social media platforms. The new 'commons' is the internet, which has been used both effectively, and nefariously, to shape public opinion, and subsequently, public policy. The relentlessness of 24/7 news cycle has bombarded us with images of war, famine, pandemic statistics, civil unrest, and violence, prompting strong emotional responses to crises that are not within our control.

In his introduction, Turner sets himself the task of exploring the changing nature of religion's influence on civil society, and argues from the outset that "we are moving into a period of incivility associated with: political extremism, populism, the erosion of citizenship, and the corruption of elites."

He outlines how religion has traditionally been considered to have been a uniting and guiding force in shaping culture, economics, politics, and social life. He references the multi-dimensional nature of religion which includes religious beliefs and practices, as well as religious feelings, religious knowledge, and religious effects. We are also reminded of how religion has been used for good: driving positive transformational agendas, and for evil: to destroy institutions, societies, nations, and to damage the world.

Turner then poses this question:

> Is religion part of the problem, or part of the solution of democracy?

When we witness political leaders appealing to one religious group to the detriment of others, we can understand why some people argue that a thriving democracy requires that religion be eliminated, that somehow 'pure' and 'rational' decisions can be made on the basis of 'facts'. While our frame of reference is Christianity and Western democracies, this argument is equally true of Muslim-majority democratic countries. Returning to

Turner's question, we actually need to ask ourselves a different question: Is the impact of religion on democratic participation really declining or is it manifesting itself differently in secular times?

The most interesting part of Turner's essay, for me, has been his analysis of the influence of neoliberalism on society, and how, in turn, this has impacted on mainstream religion. His suggestion that decades of economic rationalism, new public management theory and practice have shaped how individuals perceive their place in the world, and fundamentally changed the place of organized religion within democracies, rings true. It is political ideology, not secularism, that has changed society, and has impacted on mainstream religion. Turner cites the *Marriage Amendment Act 2017* as a law to bring the churches into line with secular society, to support his argument that religion has become part of the global economic system.

By drawing on a wide range of contemporary events and examples, Turner has created a cogent argument that our communal life has shrunk; that we are consumers of both economic and religious goods and services; that our everyday life has become increasingly commodified; and that our decision-making has become more secular. He bases his arguments on consideration of eight broad issues: social diversity and religious differences, multiculturalism, citizenship, secularisation, civil society, social solidarity, capitalism, and the relationship between church and state.

Turner suggests "that the forces that are changing and eroding citizenship and democracy are the same forces that are changing and undermining religion". Is he right?

The disruption of Covid-19 provides a challenging context in which to consider this suggestion. While Covid-19 has affected almost all countries across the globe grinding our social, political, and economic systems almost to a halt, it has also intruded into our spiritual domain. Despite the lingering uncertainty, Covid-19 silently offers us an opportunity to reflect on the spiritual impact it has on the world and our communities.

What we are discovering through the global and local responses to Covid-19 is that, while it is a worldwide threat, it reminds us that we are a global community. We're all in this together—the pandemic is everyone's problem, no one has escaped its impacts; it has stopped wars and opened prisons for thousands of dissidents. It has triggered global efforts to develop a vaccine, and international cooperation to share medical aid, expertise, and supplies between countries.

Covid-19 has also created public policy crises as jobless numbers rise, businesses have collapsed, and whole sectors of economies have been shut down by the social distancing measures that are being enforced. Industries and communities are in crisis when their economic base has disappeared. Yet, people have been compliant. What we are witnessing is that controlling the virus largely rests on a unified response from the general population for the time being. So, Covid-19 demands physical distancing but also requires unified societal action.

In their work around translation as a form of cross-cultural communication, the Russian academics, Evgeniia Erenchinova and Elena Proudchenko, write that spiritual values are "creative and constructive mechanisms working to stabilise the society, to prevent its destruction, this is their regularity."[2] We are witnessing this in responses to Covid-19. Compassion, kindness, sympathy, and caring are some of those spiritual values that drive humanity in its basic form. Often these values get overshadowed in our intellectual insight and striving for practical wisdom.

The pandemic is changing our lookout towards others in our global community. It is forcing us to be compassionate, and protect people we know, but also people we do not know or even, possibly, care about.[3] We are seeing stronger acknowledgement of the contribution of all the frontline workers who are keeping us protected, fed, and safe.

Covid-19 has also curtailed religious freedom while kindling faith. Many of us turn to prayer in a time of crisis but religious places—churches, mosques, and temples—have been closed, curtailing important rituals in our lives. For some, this loss will cause them to feel isolated and lose hope, so we have seen great 'spiritual innovation' as religious institutions have worked to stay connected and support their faithful.

So, is our communal response to Covid-19 an aberration? Is the strengthened sense of community and democracy, collaboration across sectors, social solidarity, and strong civility we are witnessing a temporary divergence from the decline that Turner articulates? We can only wait and see, if and when we return to the 'new normal', whether those values endure in 'building back better'. The gloomy economic picture which signals a deep recession is, I believe, going to challenge us all.

In re-imagining our future, Freeman's contribution focuses on how religion influences leadership in democratic societies. He recommends that all aspiring politicians should study religion, which has a "powerful sway over the formation of values" in its adherents, and a "tenacious capacity to bind people into communities of faith" because the values and institutions of religion animate the population.

Australia has been traditionally considered a Christian country. Although the growth of minority religions has increased since the mid-twentieth century, the influence of Christianity manifests itself in the varied leadership styles adopted by its political leaders: whether as democratic or autocratic leaders, servant leaders, transformational leaders, charismatic leaders, or strategic leaders. We can recognise these leadership styles in former prime ministers, and identify those who use their religious beliefs and practices to model, encourage, enable, inspire, and challenge the nation. Often, we hear the expression 'a leader for the times' as an affirmation of their effectiveness.

Freeman suggests that the decline in religious identity in Australia poses challenges for democratic leaders if and when the significance of religion becomes important only to a minority of Australians. He argues that this trend is contrary to that of the global population, where there is growth in religious identity.

Yet, in keeping with Christopher McCrudden's analysis of the three main religious traditions, where beliefs, values, practice, institutional structure, and social identity help maintain a sense of connectedness and wholeness, Freeman also acknowledges that competing religious worldviews share basic convictions about the nature of reality and morality.

Freeman references retired Justice of the High Court, J. D. Heydon, who contrasts the "elite of the Federation generation" and their deference to religious authority with "modern elites" whose indifference to religion has shifted to anti-clericalism. This critique comes at a time when the world, and most recently the whole of Australia, has been exposed to findings of sexual abuse of children and vulnerable adults, followed by the criminal findings against Cardinal Pell, which have now been struck down by the High Court. Subsequent revelations of sexual misconduct well beyond religious institutions, perpetrated by those with power and privilege, have prompted the #MeToo movement, and, ironically, have implicated Heydon himself and the legal fraternity in Australia.

Heydon is critical of the decline in rationality that is evident in the increasingly secular arguments of modern elites. We need only consider the leadership of President Trump to recognise that abandoning rationality and shifting to propaganda and oratory is a political device effectively being used to assuage those most affected by the declining economic and social influence of America in the world. Trump is using his personal wealth and political capital to tap into the emotional state of the nation, by using the rhetorical devices that are associated with religious traditions, including "the quest for consolation in an inhospitable world" to support his aspiration for re-election as President.

Freeman acknowledges that there are practical imperatives for political leaders to accommodate the religious difference (and indifference) of the Australian population, an issue I have briefly alluded to in my earlier comments about the Parliamentary Christian Fellowship. Trump's regular use of 'thoughts and prayers' has devalued that expression in the public's mind. The use by the prime minister, Scott Morrison, who *is* a person of faith, of that expression during the ravaging bushfires was criticised as glib, by those who wanted to see immediate action on the ground in support of shattered communities. Since then, he has replaced what could be construed as religious sentiment, with more nuanced references to 'healing, hope, and recovery'.

Freeman introduces Sandel's notion of 'the encumbered self' to explain how we differentiate between conscience and choice: "where conscience dictates, choice decides". In order to explore contemporary social issues, including those about religious freedoms contained in legislation currently before the Australian Parliament, Freeman teases out the inherent differences between ethics and morality, and how globalisation challenges our worldviews.

During the Covid-19 lockdown, while watching the BBC

series, "Years and Years", I had Freeman's essay in the back of my mind. This dystopian series, which traverses a fifteen-year period in the lives of a British family, predicts the social consequences of public policies, enacted insidiously and without conscience by a populist prime minister. From eliminating the poor and refugees, to the intrusion of AI in controlling their lives, the series creates a sense of dread about the future. But the resilience of the Lyons family, and the incidents of civil disobedience that occur, provide some consolation that the eerie forecasts of the programme could be circumvented by dismantling some of the worst excesses of political ideology and a restoration of civility and social identity.

Watching the final episode, I was reminded of Rabbi Harold Kushner's words:

> A world without God would be a flat, monochromatic world, a world without colour or texture, a world in which all days would be the same. Marriage would be a matter of biology, not fidelity. Old age would be seen as a time of weakness, not of wisdom. In a world like that, we would cast about desperately for any sort of diversion, for any distraction from the emptiness of our lives, because we would never have learned the magic of making some days and some hours special.[4]

The inadequacy of relativism, explored so well by Freeman, is brought to life in "Years and Years", which, through its subtle (and not so subtle) narrative, highlights the importance and dignity of difference, that there is no universal truth, and that it is through belonging that we make sense of our lives.

Freeman's conclusion that religious belonging is a social asset rather than a social liability is one that is made evident in our current political discourse. A recent joint letter from Australia's religious leaders to the Australian Government acknowledged the shared responsibilities for sustaining Australia's wellbeing through the pandemic and coming economic crisis.

In conclusion, then, what is the answer to the original question posed by Bryan Turner? Is religion part of the problem, or part of the solution of democracy? The answer surely is—it's a little bit of both.

These essays provide valuable insights into the philosophical challenges for modern leaders. They are each highly provocative in highlighting that the ethical and visionary aspects of leadership align with religious-based beliefs and values. Where religion and leadership converge in democratic governance, they provide insights into the future, based on past and present realities. Where religion is absent, those insights will surely be destructive and misunderstood.

4

Faith's place in an age of democratic trial

Robert W. Hefner

BRYAN TURNER AND DAMIEN FREEMAN have provided us with timely and insightful reflections on the deeply contested place of religion in nations around the world, not least in Western liberal democracies. Both essays remind us that most moderns today live in societies where (to use Turner's apt phrase), "The original certainty that modernity meant secularisation and secularism has disappeared, but it is unclear what is in its place." Invoking a cultural legacy that looks back to Alexis de Tocqueville,* Turner and Freeman also rightly

---

* As Bryan Turner explains in his essay, Alexis de Tocqueville was a French aristocrat who travelled to the United States in 1831 and discovered to his surprise that Protestant congregationalism was the "first institution" of American democracy. In particular, de Tocqueville observed, participation in small-town congregational assemblies was where many Americans learned the "habits of the heart" so central to American democracy, including its qualities of volunteerism, civil dialogue, and shared leadership. In the aftermath of the Cold War, as political scientists scrambled to determine just what circumstances in society are conducive to democracy's flourishing, analysts like the Harvard political scientist, Robert D. Putnam, drew on de Tocqueville's insights to argue that a dense network of participatory associations is a key to "making democracy work" in all societies. The resulting neo-Tocquevillian revival was a key feature of academic and policy discussions of democracy during the 1990s. By the end of the decade, however, the growth of religiously and racially discriminatory associations in Western Europe and other areas of the world led many analysts to temper their Tocquevillian enthusiasms. They came to realise that not all

underscore that certain varieties of religion played a central role in laying the foundations for democracy and civil society in what were to become Western liberal democracies. Against this backdrop, Turner and Freeman pose a question of singular but troubling importance: In a "secular age",[1] when widely shared religious convictions can no longer be taken for granted, and where the forces of globalisation, new social media, and populist mobilisation put citizenship and civility in question, on what social and moral sensibilities can citizens depend to determine just who they are and "what really matters" in private and public life?[2]

Turner and Freeman offer related but subtly different diagnoses of the broader causes of our crisis of citizenship and collective conviction. In this essay, I want to join the dialogue they have so ably initiated, highlighting the insights they offer, but also situating their diagnoses in a robustly comparative context. My overriding concern here is the thesis presented in Bryan Turner's essay, "that the forces that are changing and eroding citizenship and democracy are the same forces that are changing and undermining religion." I think that thesis is both correct and critically important for anyone interested in religion and democracy in the world today. Where my essay will attempt to offer additional materials for reflection will be with regard to the precise nature of the forces that are transforming citizenship and religion, and what, if anything, can be done to diminish their more damaging effects. I agree, in particular, that late-modern processes of individualisation are corroding the solidarities on which both democracies and religion depend. However, other

associational life is "good" for democracy—particularly where the association in question promotes a public ethical culture that discriminates against outsiders or certain categories of social actors (religious and racial minorities, etc.). See R.W. Putnam, *Making Democracy Work: Civic Traditions in Modern Italy* (Princeton University Press, 1993), and R.W. Hefner (ed.), *The Politics of Multiculturalism: Pluralism and Citizenship in Malaysia, Singapore, and Indonesia* (University of Hawaii Press, 2001).

processes are also thickening new forms of association and self-identification; often, however, they do so in ways that exacerbate social polarisation and undermine the civilities on which liberal democracy depends. All this is to say that I believe Turner and Freeman have got it right, but things may be even more complicated than their powerful analyses suggest.

Several years ago, the late great political scientist, Alfred Stepan, contributed a chapter to a book on *Rethinking Secularism* addressing some of the questions with which Turner and Freeman are concerned. Stepan opened his essay by pointing out that theorists of democracy in the early post-war period, including Arend Lijphart and Juan Linz, never assumed that a "strict separation of church and state" was required for a society to undergo democratisation.[3] "Democratic institutions do need sufficient political space from religion to function,"[4] Stepan added, but the forms this institutional separation has taken even in Western liberal democracies are more varied than the "separatist pattern" characteristic of state-society-religion relations in late twentieth-century United States and France. Beyond the latter two countries' "assertive secularist" separation of religion and state,[5] religion and democracy in other Western settings co-evolved in notably less separatist circumstances. One such setting was that associated with the "'established religion' pattern dominant in such twentieth-century democracies as Sweden, Denmark, and Norway"; the second was the "'positive accommodation' pattern . . . prominent in such democracies as the Netherlands, Belgium, Switzerland, and Germany."[6] In all of these settings, there was a *relative* separation of religious and state institutions, but not of the assertive sort seen in the United States or France; nonetheless, democratic institutions and citizenship still took hold. Notwithstanding these historical realities, in policy and academic circles in the United States, the Franco-American pattern of assertive secularism is still today often assumed to be "normatively preferable and empirically predominant" within modern democracies.[7] But in historical reality no such empirical predominance ever prevailed. Indeed, in another incisively comparative assessment of the separation of religion and state (SRAS) around the world, this one in 152 nations, the political scientist Jonathan Fox has demonstrated that if we define a "strict interpretation of SRAS" as "no state support for religion and no state restrictions on religion, no state has full SRAS except the United States."[8]

All this is to suggest that, just as Turner and Freeman argue, democracy in the West and in other areas of the world has emerged in varied circumstances—not just of high-wall separatist secularism, but often of extensive but un-totalising collaboration across the religion-state divide. Stepan provided some additional indices of this historical fact. He pointed out, for example, that every country in the European Union, including France, provides funding for religious education. Some 89% of European Union countries allow religion courses in state schools; 44% provide some measure funding for clerical salaries; 37% collect taxes for churches; and almost one in five have officially recognised 'state' religions.[9]

The evidence Stepan, Fox, and others have offered to illustrate that democracy has evolved in circumstances entirely different from those assumed in simplistic varieties of secularisation theory confirms a core premise of Turner and Freeman's essays. But their arguments take us even further, reminding us of the important Tocquevillian thesis that (to quote from Turner's essay) "a vibrant civil religion is an important foundation for democracy"; this is the case because it is within "religious chapels, congregations, or communities," as well as in other voluntary associations, "that citizenship and civility are fostered and nurtured." Freeman makes a related and equally important point, noting that it was "the Christian religion that introduced the notions of the inherent value and fundamental equality of all human beings, which are central to any form of liberalism."

Here again, I would suggest, Turner and Freeman get the facts right. Both are also right to emphasise that many assertive secularists in Western democracies have forgotten religion's vital contribution to democracy and citizenship. While agreeing with their general thesis, I think it might also be useful to complicate the details of the Turner-Freeman argument just a bit. It is not just indifference to matters of religion that has led secularist-minded people in liberal democracies to forget religion's contribution to public life and citizenship. The recognition has been occluded by the fact that the 'Tocquevillian' contribution to modern Western democracies has always had the potential to be double edged: inculcating in many people habits of the heart vital to civic participation and egalitarian recognition, but instilling in others the confidence that those who do not share a particular religious, ethnic, or ethical background are somehow less than full and equal co-citizens.

To explain this point let me return for a moment to another historical dimension of religion in Western liberal societies, one that is sometimes overlooked in more optimistically Tocquevillian readings of religion and democracy. What I am referring to here is a point raised in several recent studies of Christianity in liberal democracies, including another article by Jonathan Fox.[10] In the latter essay, Fox reviews a broad range of facts on state-society-religion relations around the world, this time in Christian-majority democracies in Western Europe, Latin America, and Eastern Europe. Fox points out that about thirty of the forty countries that meet his criteria for being Christian-majority and stable democracies managed to develop their democracies under circumstances where the state favored either one Christian church over all other religions (40% of the sample) or several Christian denominations (and sometimes also Judaism) over other religions. In 87.5% of Fox's Christian democratic sample, course instruction in Christianity is offered in public schools; however, only a tiny minority among the Christian democracies offer the same option for non-Christian students. More ominously, Fox notes, "religious discrimination is ubiquitous in Christian democracies", as expressed in restrictions on the ability of minorities to build places of worship, bring in foreign clergy, or otherwise enjoy a freedom of religious expression on par with that of their Christian co-citizens.[11]

In his 2009 study of the history of secularism in modern France, Turkey, and the United States, the San Diego-based political scientist, Ahmet Kuru, sheds a similar light on the Janus-faced reality of religion and citizenship, this time with regard to Protestantism and democracy in the United States. Kuru recognises and celebrates the Tocquevillian truism that, at the dawn of the republic, participation in congregational life was one of the first institutions of American democracy. Drawing on historical and sociological studies, however, he then goes on to remind us that some American Protestants in the nineteenth and early twentieth centuries invoked this same fact to make a less inclusive claim in American politics and public culture, asserting that all those citizens who were not Protestant and not white were in fact not full and equal American citizens. Notwithstanding the First Amendment's strict separation of church and state, "Protestant quasi-establishment"[12] became the informal reality of American civil religion from the early 1800s onward. A generic, King-James-Bible-based variety of Protestantism was mandated in public-school curricula, with the express aim of "acculturating students with non-denominational Protestantism"; "the public schools' curricula were rife with material that Catholics and Jews found offensive."[13] As the Catholic proportion of the population swelled from 35,000 in 1780 to 3,000,000 in 1860, anti-Catholic and antisemitic nativism surged as well. When Catholics responded to Protestant bias in public schools by appealing for state funding for their own schools, Protestants replied by pressing for a constitutional amendment banning funding to 'sectarian' schools. When the Congress failed to pass the proposed legislation, a similar amendment was added to the constitutions of thirty-seven states.[14] Outside the state in 'civil' society, the nativist surge often took an even more exclusive and violent turn, as in the epidemic of violence unleashed by groups like the Ku Klux Klan.[15] Between 1880 and 1920, as the Catholic population grew to more than 17,000,000 people (of some 92,000,000 total), the official legislative supports for exclusivist enactments of Protestant quasi-establishment were challenged and gradually removed. But informal discrimination and even violence remained widespread, now often targeting African Americans and non-Christian minorities as well as Catholics.

By my reading, none of these reminders of the uncivil side of religion's Janus-face detract from the fact that key features of religion in the modern West contributed to the inculcation of civil habits of the heart, as well as providing theological and ontological grounds for the affirmation of human dignity. Even in the mid-to-late nineteenth century, non-nativist currents in American Protestantism played a central role in the struggle against slavery and its Jim Crow legacy in the aftermath of the Civil War; similar currents contributed vitally to the struggle for women's right to vote. But there are more general lessons from these examples of instances when religious identities are mobilised to exclude. The first is that, even as some social and theological realities in Christianity and other world religions provide a richly encumbered grounding for human equality, other religious meanings and practices can be drawn up into a crude identity politics that aims to promote a citizenship differentiated along religious, racial, or gender lines. In a recent and important study, the African-American sociologist, Jean Beaman, has provided us with a vivid analysis of the intersectional nature of just such religious and racial dynamics in contemporary France. There, far-right nativists, many of them previously indifferent to Catholic realities, have learned to play a racialised and pseudo-Catholic identity politics. In so doing, they have pressed for a "differentiated citizenship" that excludes Muslims and racial minorities.[16] It goes without saying that a similar populist and identarian mobilisation of Christian and racial identities has fueled far-right politics in the United States in recent years.

We can and should go a bit further afield, however, so as to appreciate more clearly that the Janus-faced nature of religion and democracy is not something peculiar to Christianity or Western democracies alone. In India, the world's largest democracy, the rise of the majoritarian and xenophobic movement known as Hindutva (Hindu nationhood) has been the single most dramatic feature of national politics since the 1990s. It is important to recognise, however, that the Hindutva phenomenon was not the result of conservative Hindus mobilising *against* electoral democracy; "the movement has grown and come to power largely by obeying the procedures of parliamentary democracy."[17]

The Hindutva example speaks to a phenomenon seen in other late-modern democracies, including those in the West. In particular, nativist politicians have in many democracies learned to abide by the procedural norms of electoral democracy. However, these populists have done so, not for the purpose of promoting a more inclusive variety of 'democratic civility,' with its trademark affirmations of liberty, equality, and solidarity-in-difference.[18] They aim instead to mobilise religious identities for the purpose of building a new public culture that is majoritarian, exclusivist, and illiberal with regard to the rights and identities of social minorities.[18] To draw on Damien Freeman's apt reference to the Harvard ethical philosopher, Michael Sandel, majoritarian movements in places like India, Myanmar, France, and the United States *do* aspire to craft citizens with subjectivities more "encumbered" than the isolated monads of Kantian or libertarian liberalism. However, the encumbrances they seek to create do not aim to deepen commitments to an inclusive citizenship; they seek instead to stoke resentments against minorities and elites allegedly indifferent to the values and decency of the majority.[19] This use and abuse of religious tradition has unfortunately complicated the efforts of those like Turner, Freeman, and me, who wish to remind our fellow citizens of religion's deep contribution to democratic life.

In referring to examples like those I have mentioned, where a 'dark' Tocquevillianism obscures the positive role played by religious institutions in building cultures of human dignity, my point is not to confirm the new secularist mythologies with regards to religion. Both as a social theorist and a believer, I find Turner and Freeman's cautionary appeals both timely and true. In referring to the dark-side of religious (and other) solidarities in civil society, however, my argument is instead that, in discussions of 'civil' society, it is not just the strength of association that matters, but the public ethical norms to which those in religious associations dedicate themselves. If there is one lesson learned from the huge debate over civil society in the late 1980s and early 1990s, it is that, where the public ethics to which they dedicate themselves are exclusive or discriminatory, civil society networks and associations can become 'uncivil' and contribute not to the strengthening of an inclusive citizenship but to illiberal exclusions. In the 2000s, this important qualification on Tocquevillian truisms seems to have surged to the fore with a vengeance.

It is this problem to which Damien Freeman's essay speaks most directly, in particular when referring to the remarks of the former Chief Rabbi of the Commonwealth, Lord Sacks of Aldgate. Freeman evokes Sacks's argument that liberal democracies today "are ill-equipped to deal with moral challenges precisely because . . . 'they have adopted mechanisms that marginalise moral considerations' with the effect that Western politics has 'become more procedural and managerial' and increasingly 'reluctant to enact a vision of the common good'". Quoting Sacks again, Freeman sees this process of ethical erosion as having been compounded by the tendency of the free market, an "institution that has both enabled increasing prosperity and at the same time led to increasing social alienation," so as to exceed "its proper bounds and colonise areas that have a different logic and dynamic." With the market's colonisation of life worlds, Freeman observes (again citing Sacks) that the "covenantal relationships" by which individuals previously felt bound have given way to morally-thin "contractual relationships."

I think both Sacks and Freeman have it right. What I am less sure of is Sacks's suggestion that today, in a world of new and deep pluralities, it is only through participation in a covenantal community that such dignity-affirming convictions can be restored. "Once I understand that my absolute meaning is derived from belonging to my particular community, my commitment to the dignity of the other—who is created in the image of God—requires me to respect his absolute truth, which emanates from the particular community to which he belongs." The particularised pathway to the recognition of pan-human dignity is one that resonates strongly with me—both in the memory of my own Catholic upbringing, as well as my participation in the Catholic workers' movement during my late high school years in inner-city Cleveland, Ohio. But the thinning of shared life worlds about which Bryan Turner speaks in his essay is, in my opinion, both deeply real and pervasive around the world—and not just in the 'post-Christian' West. Many modern agents no longer have experiential access to a particular and specifically religious way of life—not least one with the qualities of continuity and coherence that Alasdair MacIntyre or Lord Sacks associates with religions as traditions.[21] As I have noted elsewhere, and as the anthropologist James Laidlaw has also recently argued,[22] I myself am also unconvinced by both MacIntyre and Saint Augustine's confidence that in earlier times believers always looked to religion as the ground for their virtue ethics and existential security, or, even when they did, that they experienced its truths as an integrated, non-contradictory whole.[23] As Charles Hallisey (one of the world's leading experts on Buddhist ethics) has argued with respect to Theravada Buddhism, and Shahab Ahmed (a Harvard University-based scholar of Islam, who passed away in 2015) has observed with regard to Islam,[24] many denizens of world religions experience their faith as encompassing "plural forms of ethical thought and practice," in part because the experience of faith is itself informed by other, "non-religious" moral currents or registers.[25] This plurality of ethical referents can at times create the relativist arrogance Freeman so vividly describes. Under certain circumstances, however, the plurality of ethical registers can itself be transformed into its own uniquely contemporary variety of modern ethical encumbrance.

Even in the midst of our contemporary moral crisis, it is important to remind ourselves that our late-modern age is not just one of crass consumerism or unencumbered and socially indifferent individualism. It is also an age which has witnessed an unprecedented surge of interest in the global environment, in the rights of sexual minorities, in the dignity of women in the face of rampant sexual predation, and the threat posed by the colonisation of life worlds by commercial rationalities. No less significant, some—if not all—who have rallied to certain variants of exclusivist majoritarianism, whether in Australia and the United States or India and Indonesia, have done so not just because of the seductive allure of the nativist illusion. However mistaken and destructive their dreams, some have rallied to populist assertions of nostalgia and old-order hierarchy in an effort to respond to the moral chaos of their everyday worlds. As with Mr Trump, Ms Hanson, and Mr Modi, the fact that some among the populist political entrepreneurs who have sought to exploit these sentiments have themselves only compounded the moral wreckage makes the choice of the new majoritarianism both ironic and ineffectual. But mass politics in an age of new social media, it seems, often works this unhappy way.

In short, however appealing Lord Sacks's particularistic pathway to universal human dignity, I fear the realities of our age are such that an effective response to the moral chaos of our age may have no choice than to be more plural, contemporary, and contingent. As the Canadian philosopher Charles Taylor has observed, "our present predicament is for the most part rather different than the one which generated" the culture wars of yesteryear.[26] Whereas, in an earlier age, political authority in the West and many other states "was defined and justified in cosmic-religious terms,"[27] today Western societies have become so culturally diverse as to make any such shared political theology impossible. The result is that, rather than building on a deeply shared religious cosmology, "We are condemned to live an overlapping consensus."[28]

All dreams of a restoration aside, this overlapping consensus need not be strip-mined of moral depth. The ethical dialogues and deliberations that lead citizens to affirm the modern values of liberty, equality, and dignity-in-difference may have to remain theologically and ontologically varied; but the ethical end point can be the same nonetheless. Charles Taylor reminds us that in "the kinds of societies in which we are now living in the West, the first feature that strikes us is the wide diversity not only of religious views but also of those that involve no religion."[29] It is in these commonplace circumstances "that contemporary democracies, as they progressively diversify, will have to undergo redefinitions of their historical identities, which may be far-reaching and painful."[30]

In these unsettled circumstances, some citizens will be able still to follow Lord Sacks's wise counsel, and look to particularistic communities and deep theologies to affirm the human universal. Others will make their way to a similar recognition through a different, more plural pathway. But that plurality in commonality need not doom us to ethical impoverishment or relativist obfuscation. With proper dialogue and dedication, our late-modern predicament can lead people of diverse conviction to affirm the importance of an encumbered and democratic selfhood even within the circumstance of only modestly overlapping truth claims.

5

Democracy in a religious world or religion in a democratic world?

Jocelyne Cesari

DAMIEN T. FREEMAN AND BRYAN S. TURNER take on the challenge of our current times: that is, the relations between democracy and religion. Their subtitle is intriguing: "Democracy in a religious world". If published twenty-five years ago, it would have read "religion in a democratic world".

Their inverted formulation reflects the growing awareness of the religious dimension of contemporary politics, which has become more and more acute, from religiously based political movements to the crisis of secular democracies. Their two essays have the virtue of refusing the either/or positions that dominate the scholarship: i.e. religion is a major cause of conflict and political violence or religion is proxy for other critical root causes: economic deprivation, imperialism, etc.

Bryan Turner's essay examines the modern relationship between democracy and religion, and the current challenges facing each.

He posits that religion and democracy are nowadays facing the same challenges: political extremism, white extremism, violent masculinity, volatile international relations, and the current Covid-19 pandemic. Turner does not treat democracy and religion, or state and church, as two separate entities. He points out that the individual is a consumer of both secular and religious goods and services. In his view, individualism is one of the main challenges to the traditional concept of religion and religious communities and practices.

In his essay, Damien Freeman focuses on the issues that secular democratic leaders, particularly the Australian ones, will face in the future to understand the importance of religion both for the religious citizens in their country of all denominations and in the world as a whole. He argues that religion is key to comprehending the society over which democratic leaders govern but that they are in general ill equipped to rise to the task. As an example, he discusses the concept of 'modern elite' coined by the former Justice of the High Court of Australia, J. D. Heydon, in opposition to "intolerant and irrational" religious groups. This polarisation between modernity and politics on the one hand and religion and intolerance on the other hand, is revelatory of the lack of understanding so common among Western political elites and Australian ones in particular.

Both papers draw a nuanced picture of the influence of religion on politics and vice versa and consider several factors from civility to ethics to understand their mutual influence. Building on their premises, my essay aims to address the following question: How do we move from the argument *that* religion matters to a sound theoretical and methodological approach to investigate *how* it matters? Based on my research, the response to such a question is twofold.[1] Counterintuitively, the relevant theory was articulated two centuries ago by the founders of sociology who highlighted the religious dimension of any community. The methodology is more challenging since it requires a processual rather than a variable-centered approach.

Turner discusses how individualism and the freedom of choice—a foundational concept of liberal democracies—are currently being applied to religion in a manner that undermines the formation and benefits of communities normally associated with religion, such as congregations, clubs, and other social groups. This is because, in his view, modern religion takes on the form of a supply-side model, in which it thrives when the supply is more diverse and varied, as it is the case in liberal democracies. The rise of individual spirituality has resulted in people being able to find their own religious interpretations through online debates and a wide range of options available to them for their own personal worship. Turner considers that this rise of individual spirituality as a negative effect on the social functions of religious communities. In accordance with de Tocqueville's views, Turner argues that communalism is the basis of civil society, and the decline of communal religion in association with accompanied a decline in the civility of modern society.

In my own work, I have shown that this decline of 'communal' religion is a long standing process intrinsically associated with secularisation. The end of the Wars of Religion, and the rise of the state as the central political actor, was the foundational moment of separation of religion and politics that led to the marginalisation of the societal status of religion, which is more encompassing than the civil activities of religious groups. Societal refers to the capacity of religion to shape the political community. From this perspective, religion is, at its foundation, 'politics' in the Aristotelian sense. In other words, the initial goal of religion is to provide rules and meanings for the polis or community.

As stated by Aristotle, man is a 'political animal' because he or she cannot live outside a community. In this initial meaning, politics and community, from household to family, are synonymous. The polis is the fundamental collective unit. Politics is therefore the management of that unit and religion is intrinsic to it. Nonetheless, this political status of religion has disappeared from our intellectual horizon in the modern era. We increasingly neglect or downplay the fact that religious messages are enshrined in symbols, institutions, rituals, and doctrines that aim at the creation and preservation of a specific community which sometimes overlaps and sometimes clashes with the political community. The Hindu, Buddhist, Orthodox, and Muslim visions of community entail definitions of right and wrong, of unity and solidarity, *for a group rather than persons*. It is, therefore, ineluctable that these conceptions intersect with alternative ones based on other worldviews, secular or otherwise.

In these interactions, power distribution ultimately determines the transformative capacity of one conception of community over the other. Notwithstanding this fact, the limited scholarship on the relationship between religion and power is puzzling. Such an omission is even more troubling if we bear in mind that early social scientists recognised the importance of religion for the creation and reproduction of power systems. It is worth recalling that the founder of sociology, Emile Durkheim, worked primarily on the social and political dimensions of religion.[2]

The absence of the religious dimension of political community (and vice versa) which dominates the modern epoch is partially caused by the rise of the individual as the principal recipient of the religious message. Our Western scholarship is founded on this essential division of religion and politics that marginalises religion as a provider of meaning and resources for the 'polis' in the Aristotelian sense of the term. However, this division is not fixed and varies from country to country and across historical periods even in the European and American 'cradles' of modernity, as exemplified by the rise since the 2000s of religiously based political groups. It is even more so in other parts of the world, where the religion/politics divide was imported with the concept of the nation-state.

From this perspective, modernisation means that the secular/religious distinction took precedence over the sacred/profane one. In Durkheim's theory of religion,[3] the sacred represents the unity of a group through collective symbols while, in contrast, the profane refers to mundane personal matters. In modern times, the sacred/profane divide has been replaced by the secular/religious one, where the secular nation is the cornerstone of the group unity while religion becomes personal spirituality. Of course, such a dichotomy is not pure, and religion can and does have social and political relevance. It nevertheless operates as an ideal. Additionally, the sacred has not completely disappeared in secular nations. It now refers to both political and religious symbols: the flag, the national anthem, memorials, places of worship and shrines, rituals, time.[4]

The interactions between the secular and the religious are, therefore, never-ending and determine the modern role of religion in politics and vice versa, which is not reflected in current social and political theories. The focus of political scientists on state/religion institutional relations has led to the misleading perception of continuity and fixity, which has been crystallised into the concept of secularism as the separation of church and state and/or state neutrality vis-à-vis religions. As a consequence, the religion/politics division is taken for granted while its origin and the ways it has been implemented influence the interactions between religion and democracy.

A brief history of the secular/religious distinction may clarify this assertion that the divide between religion and politics is a modern one. The 'secular' was a category developed within Latin

Christendom in the aftermath of the Wars of Religion. Saeculum, or 'profane time', was contrasted with eternal sacred time.[5] In Latin, 'saeculum' meant a fixed period of time, roughly one hundred years or so. In the Romance languages, it evolved into 'century'. After the Wars of Religion, it became used to contrast this temporal age of the world to the divinely eternal realm of God.[6] Anything 'secular' has to do with earthly affairs rather than with spiritual affairs.

As a consequence, certain places, institutions, persons, and functions were inscribed within one or the other 'times'. The transfer of certain properties and institutions out of church control to the state was therefore 'secularisation'. For the first time since the establishment of the Catholic Church, the political community could exist outside the divine guidance of the pope and be defined on its own terms. From this moment on, secularisation in Western Europe has never stopped, not simply at the institutional level but most importantly at the societal level, leading to today's dominant perception that 'this worldly' is all there is, and that the higher 'other worldly' is the product of the human community. After the War of Religions, the church delegated its guidance of the immanent to the political power. This division of labour was the invention of Latin Christendom and, incidentally, constituted Christendom's contribution to the process of secularisation.[7] The Western understanding of the secular builds on this separation. It affirms in effect, that the 'lower' immanent or secular order is all that there is and that the 'higher', or transcendent, order does not exist to regulate the 'lower'. This separation was accelerated through the Reformation, laying the groundwork for the ascendance of a neutral, self-sufficient, secular order, and leading to the contemporary situation where belief in God is considered to be one among several viable spiritual options. Simultaneously, the nation became the superior collective identification that took precedence over religious allegiances, which from now on could only be acceptable without political power. Religion became the domain of personal spirituality while all collective allegiances were oriented toward and subdued to the nation as a sovereign community of individuals equal in rights. From this perspective, the five commitments laid out by Freeman as central to a religious worldview, and especially the emphasis on transcendence, are in fact the outcome of this confinement/relocation of religion exclusively on the vertical or transcendental axis. This commitment to transcendence manifests itself not only in individuals' behaviours but also in institutions as well, which indeed can create tensions with secular institutions.

Regretfully, most of our theories of social sciences do not allow us to capture this complexity. For example, modernisation has been defined as the separation between 'this worldly' and the 'other worldly', relegating religion to personal faith and beliefs with no direct implication on society and politics and therefore secondary, if not inconsequential, to serious research. The problem is that this relegation does not reflect the reality of religion in advanced secular democracies as discussed by Turner and Freeman. For example, the problems facing both modern religion and modern democracy— extremism, opposition to multiculturalism, violent masculinity, etc—also add to this negative effect. The rise of such alienating and extremist views destabilises democracies. To further exacerbate the issues, extremist values and the conservative values of religious groups often overlap, such as the strict gender roles in both violent masculinity and Evangelical Christianity. The outcome has been a decrease of civility in modern society, going against the tenet of *civil* debate as a central theme of democracy. In the same vein, it is difficult for Heydon's 'modern elites' to understand religious worldviews when these elites are not familiar with the hardship and suffering that so many religions are focused on relieving. As noted by Freeman, they are also unable to grasp Michael J. Sandel's concept of the 'encumbered self', in which an individual is obligated to a duty that comes from a higher power. This is because the 'encumbered self' goes against the liberal democratic concept of personal freedom and individuality and makes religious freedom into a matter of obligation rather than choice.

The discrepancy between political reality and our theoretical tools is aggravated by the fact that the triad modernisation-privatisation-democratisation has served as the golden standard of political development outside the West. For this reason, the classification of religious forms of life in political science casts them almost exclusively as ideological phenomena, that is identified and studied primarily as ideas or beliefs. Such an approach reduces religion to rhetoric for political mobilisation and gives the illusion that the knowledge of concepts and symbols in religious traditions is the principal or only way to understand their role in politics. Scholarship in theology and the study of religion that gives pre-eminence to textual analysis has reinforced that tendency and contributed to decontextualised approaches to religion as if ideas or beliefs alone determine political situations. As a consequence, two other dimensions of religion (belonging and behaving) are neglected in the political analysis, while they are in some cases more significant than the belief.

Consequently, the analysis of the never-ending interactions between religion and politics is challenging, if not impossible, within existing political theories. As an alternative, I have proposed to identify sites of particular tensions which continuously redefine what is politics and what is religion across periods of time, national contexts, and religious traditions.[8] This approach focuses on processes of interaction rather than fixed features operationalised in variables. I shall provide a few examples of such a perspective by revisiting the case of Islam in Europe discussed by Bryan Turner.

One of the reasons for the contestation of the religious legitimacy of Islam in Europe is the tensions between conflictual modes of secularisation. In Europe, secularisation, as discussed above, led to a distinction of public and private, with a relegation of most religious manifestations in the second realm. Muslim immigrants, however, come from countries where Islamic references are central to collective national identities, even in secular countries like Turkey. The disjunction between private convictions and public behaviours relates to the personal and social behaviours of citizens in public space. This distinction is the result of what sociologist of religion Charles Taylor calls the mutations of the Western secularisation process mentioned earlier. These mutations led to two major changes: first, the concept of good political order and social virtues was disconnected from Christian ethics; second, the world became divided between the immanent and the transcendent. This divide was the invention of Latin Christendom and, incidentally, Christendom's contribution to the secularisation process.[9] The new understanding of the secular builds on this separation. It affirms, in effect, that the 'lower' (immanent or secular) order is all that there is and that the 'higher', or transcendent, is not to regulate the 'lower'. So, a believer in the transcendent is expected to keep it to himself and not let belief influence the political or social practices in which he engages. This is the foundational principle of the difference between private convictions and public behaviours.[10]

When Muslims settle as citizens within the public spaces of Europe, their behaviours do not conform to that private/public disjunction. The reason does not lie in the Islamic religion per se but in the status of Islam within the national communities from where these Muslims are coming.

Nation-building in Muslim countries resulted in a decisive re-organization of the society-state-religion nexus, unknown in premodern times, since, under the Caliphates, Islamic institutions and clerics were not subordinate to political power—since these clerics were financially and intellectually independent from the former.[11] The Caliphs also acknowledged the cultural and religious diversity of the population, although it did not translate into an egalitarian legal and political status for all religions and ethnicities. The *ummah* was defined as the sum of the territories and populations under the Caliphate rule, hence encompassing an extensive distribution of ethnic, cultural, and linguistic groups, including: Muslims, Christians, Jews, Zoroastrians, Bahais, and Druzes. Even though the Caliphate represented the original community which follows the message of the Prophet Mohammad, in reality, its power was transformed by geography and historically evolved into a secular dynasty overseeing multiple ethnic and religious groups.[12]

As the Ottoman Empire collapsed, the emergence of the state as the central political institution went hand-in-hand with the homogenisation of the populations inhabiting the nation's territory. That is why nation-building systematically omitted and sometimes eradicated particular ethnic, religious, and linguistic groups in order to create one nation defined by one religion and one language. This homogenisation process also led to a politicised narrative of religion, i.e. what I call political Islam. With the rise of the nation-state, a congruence was created between Muslims of a certain obedience (for example, Maleki, Shafi'i, Hanbali, and Hanafi schools) and bounded territory. Shari'a, previously the monopoly of ulemas, was reshaped as state law and secularised with the introduction of French or British legal procedures. It was also reduced to family law (marriage, divorce, custody of children, and inheritance), while Shari'a courts were abolished and replaced by a secular court system. Because of the lasting role of Islam in regulating these dimensions of the immanent (family life, sexuality, freedom of speech), they are nowadays the most acutely disputed issues between secular and religious actors. In other words, the ulemas lost their influence on the immanent and were progressively relegated into the management of souls or family affairs. Hegemonic Islam occurred in three major ways:

1) the nationalisation of institutions, clerics, and places of worship of one particular trend of Islam (for example Sunni over Shia);

2) the redefinition and adjustment of Shari'a to the modern legal system as well as inclusion of Islamic references into civil law (marriage/divorce), criminal law, and as restriction of freedom of speech (blasphemy/apostasy), based on the prescriptions of that particular brand of Islam; and

3) the insertion of the doctrine of that religion into the public school curriculum beyond religious instruction, that is in national history textbooks and civic education.

All Muslim states have put some elements of Islamic law in the secular state and have adopted Islam as the main regulator of national identity (except Indonesia, Senegal, and Tunisia post-Jasmine Revolution). For these reasons, in Muslim-majority countries, Islam is seen as a marker of national and collective identity independently of the level of personal religious practice, not only for Muslims but also for religious minorities.

It is, therefore, not surprising that Muslims have imported this specific private/public divide, which inevitably clashes with the dominant European one, when they settle in Western Europe. In this respect, most of the controversies surrounding Islam in secular Europe relate to three major manifestations of the private/public disjunction: secular justification, primacy of individual rights over collective rights, and effacement of the religious self in public space. Muslims are perceived as at fault because they seem noncompliant to the principle of secular justification; they privilege collective rights over individual rights; and they bring the religious self in public space.

First, most of the recent crises related to Islam in public space can be interpreted as a critique that Muslims are unable or unwilling to conform to this principle of secular justification. For example, the Rushdie affair can be read as Muslims' difficulty in complying with the principle of secular justification.[13] In this sense, the condemnation of the *Satanic Verses* and the push by some Muslims to have the book banned highlight the challenge posed by the disjunction between private convictions and public behaviours of the 'immanent frame'. Additionally, some Muslims have not built a strong 'buffered self',* and, therefore, are unable to accept that individual rights and freedom of religion can operate independently of religious convictions. Second, the recognition of Islamic law within existing legal systems, and the concern that specific subcultures can stifle individual rights, is another example of the tension between political order and Muslim communities.[14] Third, some Islamic religious practices entail bodily prescriptions (dress code, dietary rules) that have been eroded from Christian practices through the European secularisation processes described above. Other religious populations in Europe, like Jews, have also experienced these transformations, although some groups, like ultra-Orthodox or Haredi, display strong commitment to embodied religious behaviours. To be clear, Islam also underwent a secularisation process in Muslim-majority countries, but it has retained public displays of praxis that are, therefore, now globalised through increased migration and circulation of persons and ideas.[15]

These readjustments of the religious dimension of political communities are also happening within the Christian groups in Europe with the rise of civilisationism and nativism. In this particular case, it is not the behaving but the religious belonging that is mobilised

---

* In Charles Taylor's terminology, the buffered self was separated and protected from "a world of spirits and forces which [could] cross the boundary of the mind" as a result of the Reformation. In short, this separation helped develop the sense that a society itself could reform as a whole if properly disciplined. In other words, the construction of the buffered self is still a work in progress, especially in a context where religious voices and orthodoxy are transnational: C. Taylor, *A Secular Age*, p. 300.

to show allegiance to the national community. Political scientist Roger Brubaker has qualified these movements as national-populist, meaning the idea of 'us' versus 'them' exists in two dimensions. In the horizontal dimension, the division is between insiders ('people like us') and outsiders, who threaten our security and way of life. In the vertical dimension, the division is between the ordinary, hard-working, virtuous people and the corrupt, self-serving, out-of-touch elite. Populism in Western Europe is distinctive in that it explains the 'us' versus 'them' divide in broader civilisational terms. Nationalism is being redefined with more weight being placed on civilisational differences like religious tradition instead of national differences like language. In secular Western Europe, Christianity is not embraced as a religion, but as a civilisational identity in direct opposition to Islam, or a way to define 'us' relative to 'them'. Secularism is used to decrease the visibility of Islam in the public domain, while liberalism (e.g. gender equality, freedom of speech) is selectively embraced as 'our' way of life in contrast to the innately illiberal Islam. Brubaker explains, "The seemingly contradictory joining of Christianism, secularism, and liberalism by the national-populist right, in short, is explained by the overarching preoccupation with Islam as an alien and threatening civilisation."[16]

To capture democracy in a religious world, religion is better deciphered through the three Bs: *belief, behaviour,* and *belonging*— an approach which is familiar to scholars of religion (who use it primarily to analyse personal levels of religiosity). What is less obvious is, on the one hand, how to apply these three Bs to collectives or groups rather than individuals, and, on the other hand, how to utilise them for *both* political and religious communities. In fact, national communities are also shaped by the three Bs: they are built on a belief (ideology), a sense of belonging to the people bounded by the same territory, and the necessity to behave according to the rules that regulate this community. The interaction between the two sets of three Bs, religious and political, can explain the politicisation of religion and vice versa in specific contexts. By investigating the intersection between the three Bs of political *and* religious communities, it is possible to identify not only how religion and politics interact, but also what is at the core of the competition between the two: changing behaviours, belonging, or beliefs. This method stays away from the fixed dichotomy of the secular and the political that permeates our Western theories and are applied outside the West without considering the local transformations of religious and political ideas and institutions.

In sum, religion and democracy can be analysed by identifying processes rather than causality and paying attention to changes in time and space of ideas and actors as well as of institutions. It is probably easier said than done in a time when sociology and political science have taken an unhistorical turn.

6

Religious freedom in the twenty-first century

David N. Saperstein

T HE TRENCHANT, INSIGHTFUL, AND PROVOCATIVE ESSAYS of Bryan Turner and Damien Freeman, which are at the core of this book, effectively illuminate central challenges regarding religious freedom both in the context of Australia and on the global scene. As they present the mix of the internationally recognised rights of religious freedom and the particular cultures of the world's varied nations, ethnicities, and religions, I share their passionate commitment to the importance of religious freedom as well as their sense of the distinctiveness of religious freedom. But neither from my legal nor religious perspectives, do I always get to their conclusions by the same, somewhat communitarian, path Freeman, and I think Turner, seem to take. Nor do I accept their sharp distinction (prominently argued by noted contemporary philosopher Michael Sandel, who is discussed at some length) between that path and a more traditional rights-oriented approach. I think the challenge is how to better meld the two. And throughout this essay, I offer perspectives and insights from the American model, from the Jewish legal tradition, and from the international perspective out of my experience engaging with religious, government, and civil society leaders in the thirty-five countries I visited while working on these issues for the Obama administration (and with those from many other nations at the United Nations and at varied international conferences).

Professor Turner discusses the 'rational choice' model of religion, arguing that "once the religious market is freed from state regulation, consumers enjoy greater choice and variety. This interpretation explains why religion has greater vitality in the United States than in Europe." This does indeed represent one key distinctive feature of American views of religious freedom and church-state relations: the so-called 'separation of church and state.' Shaped by our founding generations with their memories of cruelties and tyrannies forged by the mix of government and church, they emphasized a separation between church and state strongly implied in the opening words of the America's Bill of Rights (enshrined in the first ten amendments of the United States Constitution) that "Congress shall makes no law respecting an establishment of religion nor prohibiting the free exercise thereof."[1] "Free exercise" clearly conveys a range of actions beyond mere belief. Taken together, the emerging sense of these restrictions on government is that government should remain neutral on religion, neither favouring religion nor disfavouring; neither supporting religion nor undercutting it. So, too, government had to be neutral on the religious exercise of individuals and religious communities.[2] Over the past two centuries, in the United States, we have built a system that protects the rights of religious believers and non-believers alike to worship, practice, educate about, share, change, and express their beliefs freely—a description that would apply as well to Australia. Religious freedom has always been at the centre of American values and our success as a nation—just as it is a vital component of our foreign policy today, the latter enjoying strong bipartisan support in the United States.

The United States promulgated a radically new vision of the implications of what religious freedom meant, founding, for the first time in history, a nation state in which your rights as a citizen would not depend on your religious identity, practices, or beliefs. That is still one of the most vital tests for the existence of true religious freedom everywhere.

At the same time, from its inception, there have been sharp differences over the meaning and domestic application of our religion clauses as well as over Thomas Jefferson's formulation of "a wall of separation between church and state."[3] Conservatives argue that the concept and application of church-state separation is somehow anti-religion and anti-God. Advocates of the separation, like myself, respond that nothing could be further from the truth. It is precisely that wall keeping government out of religion that has allowed religion to flourish in America with more people going regularly to worship, more people believing in God, and more people holding religious values central to their identity than in any other democracy (rivalled only by India), including all those that have a religion established, preferred, or sponsored by the state. Hence, Turner's observation about the religious vitality of America.

As with many of the promised rights in the United States Constitution, including its Bill of Rights, we did not immediately see their implementation. But beginning in the 1940s, the Supreme Court of the United States adopted an expansive view of both the establishment clause and the free exercise clause, adopting Jefferson's "a wall of separation" formulation. This expansive approach marked the Supreme Court's view of many freedoms: free speech, freedom of the press, civil rights, and women's rights and, even as the Court has become more conservative in more recent decades, it has affirmed more expansive LGBTQ rights. As this robust view of fundamental rights began to take shape from the 1940s to the 1960s, it was exactly at that time in the post-

World War II era that the international community, influenced by the United States Supreme Court's vision of fundamental rights, shaped the two key international documents that form the basis for our international advocacy: the Universal Declaration of Human Rights and the International Covenant on Civil and Political Rights (ICCPR).[4] Article 18 of both these documents provides for the freedom of thought, conscience, and religion, including the freedom to change religion or belief and the freedom to manifest religion or belief in teaching, practice, worship, and observance. Article 18 of the ICCPR also provides that "No one shall be subject to coercion which would impair his [or her] freedom to have or to adopt a religion or belief of his [or her] choice." However, part of this same ICCPR article allows for limitations to such freedoms when they are "prescribed by law and are necessary to protect public safety, order, health, or morals or the fundamental rights and freedoms of others." Not surprisingly, legal restrictions, coercion, discrimination, and even persecution are too often implemented in the name of one or more of these specified grounds for limiting religious freedom. In this sense, Rabbi Jonathan Sacks's *The Dignity of Difference* calls us, as I believe is implied in both Turner and Freeman's essays, to be respectful of the distinct cultures, religions, and moral codes of varied nations.[5]

Interesting issues arise as Turner's essay turns to multiculturalism. He asks, "Has multiculturalism been a success or are we a nation of parallel communities?"[6] He illustrates this dilemma by discussing the integration of the Australian Muslim community, contrasting integration versus assimilation. While all the pieces of this discussion offer important insights, I would like to understand more of what the desirable goal of a religiously tolerant Australia committed to full religious freedom would look like in terms of this question.

The American model, according to the Pew Research Center's

polls, has had a more efficacious impact in integrating Muslim migrant communities than most other democracies.[7] Over the past hundred and twenty-five years, we have seen shifts among sociologists descriptively, and politicians prescriptively, from seeing America as a 'melting pot' (in which all immigrant communities after a few generations would become just American), an idea that originated in the late 1700s and became part of the broader culture with the success of the play, *The Melting Pot*, by the popular Jewish author Israel Zangwell. This gave way to an increasing recognition that America benefits from diverse ethnic, cultural, and religious groups maintaining distinctive identities. This melded the idea of America as a mosaic or salad bowl, with the recognition that while maintaining differences, there were widely accepted civic norms that defined America.[8] In religious terms, noted sociologist Robert Bellah and others recognised that coextensive with America as the most religiously diverse nation in the history of the world, there were "civil religious" norms that had become part of the fabric of America. Bellah mentioned: belief in God; public celebrations of religious holidays; the belief that God protects America. I would add at least two others: belief in a religious prophetic witness and interfaith relations as central to the American aesthetic.[9] In return, all Americans expect that while maintaining distinct differences, they will never be subject to discrimination in employment, education, housing of public accommodations on the basis of core characteristics: race, gender, national origin, religion, age, and (increasingly) sexual orientation and gender identity.

In the wake of the Second World War, we made significant strides towards these goals. While polls told us that tens of millions still held racist and antisemitic attitudes,[10] the percentage of the population holding such views was shrinking and, more importantly, the social constraints had evolved to convey the sense that you could not really make it in American society, in its political or cultural life, if you gave expression to such ideas. Obviously, the rhythm of this progress varied greatly if you were, e.g. in the Jim Crow South during the key years of the civil rights battles of the 1940s-1960s; or whether you were talking about classic forms of racial, ethnic, or religious prejudice, or women's rights, as opposed to newer forms of protections, such as those for the disabled or the LGBTQ community. Today, we see vividly the fragility of those advances, as America, like Australia and so many other nations, has been increasingly buffeted by increases in hate crimes and hate speech that have so alarmingly spiked in America.

Indeed, in these past years, we have witnessed the explosion of hate groups mostly on the right and of hate acts against Jews, Muslims, Sikhs, gays, and women in escalating numbers.[11] We have witnessed the degradation of civil discourse, first in the dark corners of the internet and then more publicly, exacerbated by the anonymity of social media and the stamp of approval of such rhetoric by too many leaders in our nation.*

What transpired at Tree of Life synagogue, where eleven people were killed and six wounded in 2018 was the most brutal, deadly antisemitic attack in the history of America. But this is not just about antisemitism. So long as any group can be targeted for hate crimes, no group is safe, and the number of hate crimes against African Americans continually far surpasses even those targeting Jews, who, in the United States, are the target of more religious hate crimes than any other religious group.[12]

It feels that across the globe we are witnessing surges in hate speech and hate crimes. And they are linked. Hate speech, bigoted

* As Dr King said in the wake of the 1963 Birmingham church bombing, those four young girls who perished "have something to say to every politician who has fed his constituents with the stale bread of hatred and the spoiled meat of racism . . . They say to us that we must be concerned not merely about who murdered them, but about the system, the way of life, the philosophy which produce the murderer."

speech, racist speech; discourse that demeans, that demonizes, that depicts those from whom we differ as the enemy, as evil, as a danger to our nation—such violent rhetoric too often can spur violent action.

And the damage such hate crimes inflict on their victims—and on our nations—can be great and requires a national response. For hate crimes are more than mere acts of violence. They are more than murders, beatings, arsons, and desecrations. Hate crimes are nothing less than attacks on the values that are the pillars of our freedoms and the legal, political, and social guarantors of that freedom. They are a betrayal of the promise of our nations. They erode our national wellbeing. Those who commit these crimes do so fully intending to tear at the too-often frayed threads of diversity that bind us together and make us strong. They seek to divide and conquer. They seek to tear us apart from within, fomenting violence and civil discord.

What has been so extraordinary is how the religious communities of America have arisen to come together after such tragedies have occurred: Muslims cleaning up desecrated Jewish cemeteries in St Louis and Philadelphia; the president of a synagogue in Victoria, Texas, handing a set of synagogue keys to the imam of an arsoned mosque to use as long as needed and four churches doing similarly; cleaning up graffiti and vandalism; the entire community of Pittsburgh standing in solidarity with the Jewish community so tragically victimized—all of this working in broad-based interfaith coalitions that are a hallmark of America—to delegitimise hate acts and hate speech. And, we look to *all* our political, religious, cultural, and civic leaders to help in achieving this. In my work as the United States Ambassador for Religious Freedom, I have seen such interfaith cooperation in so many nations including Australia in response to threats of and acts of hatred that took place in their own communities, other communities or even in other nations.

Consider the interfaith services in across the globe, including Australia, in the wake of the Christchurch massacre of Muslims or the interfaith service in Wollongong after the Lindt Café siege in Sydney.

In my own country, part of these shifts is a reaction to the reality that has already witnessed the end of white Christian majorities in America. Consider: in 2008, 54% of the American population identified as white and Christian. Today that number has fallen to 44% of the population identifying as white and Christian.[13]

This, of course, has given fuel to America's own 'replacement ideologies,' akin to Renaud Camus's as discussed by Professor Turner. When the white supremacists marched in Charlottesville, VA in 2017 in the so-called 'Unite the Right' rally, chanting racist chants and, as they marched by the synagogue where Jews were at Sabbath prayer that morning, chanting, "Jews will not replace us," it was many Americans' first exposure to such ideas.

The challenge of accommodating Aboriginal religious beliefs and practices Professor Turner discusses, proves particularly challenging everywhere, since often these practices involve spiritual attachment to land that has been a target for development by developers, farmers, herders, roadbuilders, mineral extractors, etc. Professor Turner offers an intriguing suggestion that focusing on "Aboriginal spirituality in a secular democracy may be less onerous and challenging to the citizenry than any substantial redistribution of land or recognition of Aboriginal law." It is an idea that some advocates for Native American rights have promoted since the1970s (albeit in addition to, not instead of, legal and land restoration approaches). Congress passed, in 1978, the American Indian Religious Freedom Act. While well intentioned and espousing the right principles, the lack of enforcement mechanisms doomed its potential to truly protect Native American rights. Further, the Supreme Court has rarely embraced a robust sense of the substantial burden that violations of sacred lands impose on the Native American communities. When it did, it accepted almost any asserted government interest as sufficient to outweigh the religious freedom claims, interests that fell far short of the normally required "compelling government interest" required to constrain fundamental rights.[14]

However, adding strength to Professor Turner's suggestion, the *Native American Graves Protection and Repatriation Act of 1990* has played a key role in protecting the burial grounds and sacred objects of Native Americans. And President Clinton's 1997 executive order 13007[15] did, in fact, make some improvements in access to sacred lands and government protection of the sacred lands. But in the absence of stronger congressional legislation on Native American rights, such protections remain vulnerable. Thus, President Trump has eased the restrictions on oil and gas development on, and gas pipelines being run through, Indian lands including sacred lands.[16] And in light of the disproportionate impact of Covid-19* on Native American communities and recent

---

* Thinking more generally about Covid-19, it is true, as Turner asserts, that the Covid-19 pandemic has had a paradoxical impact on patterns of religious life. On the one hand, it is far more difficult for people to attend physically religious worship, participate in communal religious rituals, enjoy communal religious celebrations and, at challenging times, have loved ones to mourn with or to be comforted by in illness. Yet, during the developing pandemic when I was serving (2019-20) as the President of the international Reform Jewish denomination (the World Union for Progressive Judaism), I was hearing widely across the globe, as houses of worship were shifting to online programming as services, holidays celebrations, religion classes, and cultural events moved online, there were reports of increases, sometimes significant, in participants. (I found this to be true from interlocutors and colleagues in Australia as well, as in March, I was on a Jewish and interfaith speaking tour in Australia as the pandemic led to the shutting down of group gatherings). So too, as Turner discussed, it has proved particularly empowering to the elderly, whose abilities to move around and appear in-person are more restricted in general. And when people came to understand why clergy could not visit personally in most Covid-19 era circumstances, it allowed clergy to reach out and connect with more people in a given time frame than had been possible with travel to in person visits. During the 2020 Jewish High Holy Days in September and October 2020, I witnessed use of technologies that were absolutely breath-taking in quality and

exposés of the failure of law enforcement and courts to adequately protect such communities,[17] there is a renewed interest in expanding Native Americans' legal autonomy in their government-recognised communities.[18] But the limited success thus far have been primarily around using a variety of legal approaches to protect sacred rights.[19]

In his essay, Damien Freeman raises a range of related key points, many of which I agree with but have differences about the conclusions I infer he is suggesting. To mention three of them: I do believe that religion can be a strong force for social cohesion; that there is, among many secular people (elites and average citizens), a strand of cynicism about organized religion and religious adherents that drives a wedge between the religiously observant and those who do not hold religious views; and that claims that originate from religious conscience based on faith beliefs need to be as fully protected as any other fundamental human rights.

Let me address each of these three issues separately.

First, on the issue of religion as a source of social cohesion, Freeman writes, "Indeed, for a long time it was believed that social cohesion required uniform religious adherence, and difference in religious practice or belief as associated with social division and disorder." As to whether that belief proved to be accurate is debatable. Clearly religion can be powerful force for social cohesion—and can be so on many different levels. Consider: religion is unique in that it is, at once, the most local and the most global of the ways we organize our identity, our lives, our sense of community: from the local parish, mosque, synagogue, or temple to the international faith group or denomination of which we are a part.

in creating and sustaining a sense of community. While many share Turner's caution that we do not know how sustainable these gains will be, these changes from traditional forms of community do not necessarily consign religious life to "placeless spirituality" as I read the essay to suggest. Indeed, it is likely we will never go back fully to reliance only on in-person engagement and that what we have learned during the pandemic crisis will strengthen aspects of religious outreach and service to constituents.

But in reflecting on religion as a source of social cohesion and considering what guidance this gives us at a time of growing social anomie, certain complications and contradictions must also be considered—both historically and today. Certainly, there have been many countries, regions and communities, where there has historically been religious uniformity out of circumstance, which in turn has strengthened social cohesion. Throughout history, however, uniform religious adherence has frequently been forcefully imposed on segments of a population who sincerely held different views. When majority religion is then enmeshed with the coercive power of government authority, it often resulted in severe limitations on religious freedom including, in the extreme, forced conversion, criminal punishment, and ethnic cleansing. Think of Catholic oppression of Protestants in Europe and vice versa, or of the Inquisition. Think of Muslim repression of Catholics, Orthodox Christians, and Jews as *dhimmi*, as second-class citizens (albeit in medieval times, Jews generally lived better under Muslim rule than under Catholic or Orthodox rule). There have been many cases where the majority asserted that only one faith interpretation was valid and others were not just wrong, but evil. The consequent oppression often resulted in systemic abuses not just of other religions but of divergent schools of thought within the majority tradition. All of this so often has led—and will lead when it occurs today, as my experience in this field has painfully witnessed—to destabilisation rather than cohesion.

Conversely, while it is hard to think of any pre-Age of Reason country that embraced norms that today we would fully equate with robust religious freedom, there are numerous examples of periods of pluralistic and tolerant societies that manifested social cohesion despite religious diversity with varied sects of a dominant religion and with other religions. Just consider the Jewish experience: Alexandria, Egypt (200 BCE to 100 CE); the episodic flourishing of Jewish life in Babylonia for hundreds of years from 300 to 1000

CE; the so-called 'Golden Age of Spain' (in Granada and in Caliph Abd al Rahman III's Cordoba, epitomised by Hasdai Ibn Shaprut and Shmuel Hanagid); and seventeenth-century Amsterdam—all of which saw both Jewish life flourish even as Jews contributed substantially to the general society.

Secondly, as to the gap between the secular elites and the religiously observant, the theme of 'incomprehensibility', is an important idea that Freeman develops in his essay drawing on Dyson Heydon. To the extent that those who significantly shape government policy and cultural norms may not understand the notions of religious obligations and duties that go far beyond just lifestyle choices, this failure poses a significant challenge for affirming religious freedom. Yet the presumption that, among Heydon's 'modern elites' (or among those who more generally do not share religious beliefs), the notion of the lack of comprehension of the nature and power of religious obligation being widespread feels too rigid a formulation. On the one hand, there are strands of societal attitudes in most nations that are condescending to religion, indifferent to its power in the lives of so many, ignorant of its content, and uninterested in even considering the burden imposed when the state forces people to violate their own religious conscience in pursuit of some compelling interest (or just reasonable interest) of the state. And certainly, there are leaders of countries and influencers of culture (Heydon's 'modern elites') who share these views.

On the other hand, even those who are not religious themselves may have been raised in a religious family; may still have religious families, immediate or extended; may be spiritual questers in ways that do not involve organized religion but do lead to an understanding of the role that spiritual meaning plays for those in organized religion. And at least in most democratic societies, almost every educated person is likely exposed to a broader culture that is replete with religious books in bookstores, religious art in museums, religious movies, and religious music. And even our non-religious specific books, movies, television shows, and music (from rock to classical) often contain religious themes. Influencers (themselves non-religious) may well be empathetic people who fully understand the difficult choices the policies and state actions they espouse may have on those who possess deeply held religious beliefs that they feel command their lives. Rather than an incomprehensible gulf, it feels much more like a spectrum of different levels of awareness, understanding, and sensitivity to a sense of religious conscience that they themselves do not share. This opens the opportunity for meaningful dialogue and efforts to educate each other and to find common ground and compromise. By no means do I deny powerful secular aesthetics that would embody such views as Freeman addresses, but as I have travelled the globe, even in strongly secularised nations and cultures, it is rare to find in democracies overt interference with the core religious life of communities or individuals affecting their right to worship, to proselytize, to preach and teach. Yet, as a Jew, I empathise deeply with the point Freeman makes, as, in recent months, in Europe, I see democratic countries try to ban core aspects of Jewish life such as circumcision or kosher slaughtering in the name of child protection or animal rights.[20] In some cases they don't understand; in others they balance out the competing moral values differently than I do—but we must always be cautious of the human tendency that, when we lose a debate, it can only be explained by the opponent not being able to see our truth, the obviousness of which must simply be incomprehensible to them.

Freeman continues his argument by suggesting that, in contrast with religion, any relativistic approach to ethics is inadequate because it does not anchor ethics in ultimate reality. The assertion that no set of non-relativist ethics is possible without recourse to an ultimate reality is, of course, a debatable assertion. On the one hand, the ultimate reality in which I hinge my truth may be different from the ultimate reality in which another person hinges their truth—even if we arrive at the same truth. On the other, there are widely accepted ethical norms in the world that have no direct link to what would reasonably be called an ultimate reality. As Milton Konvitz has noted in his book, *Judaism and the American Idea*,[21] identifying Jewish sources of American democratic thought and of the concept of human rights (sources rooted in the Covenant with the one God—one example of the kind of ultimate reality or commanding presence that Michael Sandel calls the religious conscience that we do not choose but which our faith commands). But Konvitz acknowledges that such ideas also from sources not necessarily rooted in an ultimate reality:

> But other streams of thought have also made contributions to the development of the theory of human rights: the teachings of the Stoic philosophers regarding the inviolability of human dignity; . . . the teachings of the Roman lawyers concerning a common law of nations and peoples, the *jus gentium*; the international law principles of Hugo Grotius and Samuel von Pufendorf; the writings of the French Enlightenment . . . the stress on the inherent dignity of man that can be found in the great Renaissance writers like Erasmus and Pico della Mirandola.

Relatedly, where do the Catholic, Protestant, and Jewish varying concepts of natural law fit in to this paradigm, the natural law philosophy, as Konvitz describes, "that has had a continuous life from the time of the late Roman Empire, through Thomas Aquinas and Richard Hooker, to the present time?" Some would argue that they come from God's having granted all humanity rational thought out of which ethical norms are evolved; others that the capacity for rational thought is a natural evolution.

Thirdly, in arguing that claims that originate from religious conscience based on faith beliefs need to be fully protected, and in expressing concerns as to whether a rights oriented system of protections can achieve that, Freeman observes that in this secularised world "humility and gratitude for blessings have given way to a preoccupation with rights and entitlements." He is, of course, right. But we need both and one can argue: thankfully "gratitude for blessings" has, if not given way, made room for the schema of fundamental civil and political rights and basic entitlements. The entitlements from and rights protected by the government of, for, and by the people (to paraphrase Abraham Lincoln), help provide food for the hungry, education for the illiterate, and healthcare for the ill. So too they helped bring an end to slavery and apartheid; and they helped ensure the rights of women, people of color, the disabled, the elderly, and LGBTQ people. In the main, these benefits and freedoms did not come about from gratitude for blessings or because of the humility of the persecuted, the persecutor, or the nation in which injustices festered, but from the battle of people for rights and for entitlements. Often inspired by religious ideas of justice, peace, and equality for all God's children, including the obligation to protect and provide for the "least among us," for the widow, the orphan and the stranger—and sometimes led by religious leaders, the battle for rights and entitlements secured something that the humility and the gratitude had not provided. Across the globe the struggle for such achievements flourished within the schema of a system of universal human rights that found its way into countless constitutions and laws, and which in turn provided rights and protections to the oppressed.

At one point, Freeman acknowledges that political elites may pay homage to the role of religion and commit to protecting the space for religion to flourish when it is in their interest to do so, paraphrasing the Jesuit lawyer, Frank Brennan:

> several of the key politicians did not necessarily have a personal reverence for any organized religion. What they did have, however,

> is a practical imperative for showing reverence to God. This was because they believed that it would be easier to carry the vote of the section so the population who took religious adherence seriously . . .

He connects this dynamic of Australian Federation politics to the Elizabethan scholar Jerry Brotton's transactional idea that only the self-interest of Elizabethan-era England led to the engagement with Muslim and Jewish ideas. This seems like an odd interpretation in which Brotton conflates the reason for trade relations with Muslim countries with English society's broader engagement with Muslim and Jewish ideas. In fact, there were few if any Jews in England during Elizabeth's reign and they lived as hidden Jews, if they were there. Trade with Muslim countries, spurred by economic self-interest, may well have happened during the Elizabethan era. But the engagement with Muslim and Jewish ideas likely did not. Despite the example Brotton gives of Shakespeare humanising Shylock, such engagement did not begin to happen until later, mostly evolving in the mid-seventeenth century, when there was a resurgence of interest in Oriental studies. More scholars became acquainted with Arabic (as Brotton notes in the footnote in Freeman's essay) and more with Hebrew. Indeed, Hebrew became a classical language taught alongside Greek and Latin in British universities as well as in early universities in the United States (Yale and Harvard). Led by the scholarly work of John Selden (1584-1654) the familiarity with Hebrew and Aramaic opened up a range of classical Jewish texts that heretofore had been accessible only to a few. Rather than this field of Hebrew scholarship being a result of economic self-interest of wealthy British merchants, it was taking place in the 1640s and 1650s as Puritans and other dissenters saw the Hebrew Scriptures as a key authority to their worldview. They were making both reasoned arguments for religious tolerance and millenarian arguments justifying the return of the Jews. These would see Cromwell allowing Jews back in Britain beginning in 1656 for the first time since they were expelled in 1290. As opposed to those Jews who came with William the Conqueror in 1066 primarily to fill distinct economic and legal roles that left an imprint on the history of Anglo-American law,[22] this return occurred as much if not more for ideological reasons as for economic reasons.[23]

In developing his criticism of a rights-oriented society, Freeman puts forward Heydon's use of the idea of consolation as exemplifying the distinction between what he calls a liberal democracy with a welfare state forged in a world that has provided its citizens "food, drink, and a comfy sofa"—intended as a symbol for the economic success of many democratic countries—in contrast to the worldview of religious traditions. This attack on welfare states feels misplaced.

The notion that

> worldviews of religious traditions tend to be formed in a world in which life is more readily characterized by woe, pain, misery, hunger, and despair . . . the religious worldview maintains that there is something important about the quest for consolation that is born of an inhospitable world; and which remains of enduring importance even in a much more physically hospitable world. It is not hard to see how this thought could be incomprehensible to those who do not share it.

Again, seems to draw too stark a contrast.

The *raison d'etre* of the welfare state is to structure the communal responsibility to assist "the least among us" and to assert that they are entitled to the protections of the state even as the state creates incentives for private charity to complement those efforts. In most welfare states, social welfare efforts of the private sector (including the religious sector) and the state work together. Often the state subsidises religious communities' charitable efforts without regard to their religious beliefs. The picture of two unconnected spheres in democratic countries of modern elites and religious believers (even fundamentalist believers) only rarely reflects the reality I have found in my travels to eighty countries. This is true even in terms of consolation. I have tremendous appreciation for the role of religious institutions and clergy in bringing consolation to those who are hurting. That remains true even in secular democracies. But they do not need to shoulder that role alone. In the United States, when we think of moments requiring consolation—including 9/11, Hurricane Katrina, the Oklahoma City bombing, school shootings, and many others—it is not only America's hundreds of thousands of houses of worship and national religious leaders who provide consolation, but, as often, our political leaders like Presidents Clinton (who was particularly graceful in bringing consolation), Reagan, both Bushes and Obama, as well as state governors and mayors, who complemented the consolation provided by religious communities and leaders. I do not know, as I write, the outcome of the 2020 election in the United States, but I have known Joe Biden for forty-five years, and he too has the gift and has gone out of his way to be a consoler in times of crisis. For many of these leaders, their own role as consolers is derived from their own religious beliefs, albeit none were 'fundamentalists.' And the tremendous investment of resources to sustain those who suffer, providing food to the hungry, shelter for those who have lost their homes, care and solace to the ill, support which tends to be particularly robust in welfare states—all are forms of consolation. I do not know Australia, but I have seen Prime Ministers Tony Blair and Gordon Brown of the United Kingdom, Prime Minister Jacinda Adern of New Zealand, and Israeli President Reuven Rivlin perform such functions in a heartfelt manner. All, I presume, a combination of religious individuals and modern elites.

Freeman acknowledges that (for many of the reasons discussed above) the United States is a bit different and that looking out to

2050, 60% in United States will be Christians, compared to many other Western-style democracies, including Australia, where Christians will be a minority. I would point out, however, that overlapping with the increased secularisation of most democratic societies is the rejection of associational connections captured in the American context so vividly by Harvard's Robert Putnam in his seminal book, *Bowling Alone*. In this book, he analyses the impact of the patterns of suburbia (as opposed to urban and small town life), the breakdown of the family, the changes wrought by so many two-parent working families, the technological shifts in communications, media, and work—all of which have greatly weakened social capital and social cohesion and put enormous pressure on associational relationships, including religious associational relations.[24] But he recognises that, despite this, religion still is a source of social capital that is distinctive among Western democracies.[25] Yet, he points out that recent generations have witnessed enormous shifts in American religious life. There is not nearly the denominational loyalty that marked the nineteenth and twentieth-century era, with roughly one-third of Americans having switched religions at some point in their lives.[26] Affiliation rates may be declining, but a not insignificant percentage of those who answer "none-of the above" to polls on denominational affiliation consider themselves believers in God or spiritual questers. Putnam also shows the resulting high rates of interfaith marriages, suggesting that one third of the all marriages today are interfaith. All these changes have manifested a positive byproduct:[27] and a general interest in and willingness to strengthen interfaith action and cooperation. These links are forging new forms of social cohesion, the impact of which is difficult to assess.

Today, of course, we live in an era of interfaith relations that surpasses in numbers, scope, and depth anything in human history prior to this era. The scope and power of such efforts has greatly increased the religious literacy of key leaders in each of our societies. While we all have challenges we must face within our own faith communities, when we *can* work together, in our vast numbers we can achieve things none of us can achieve alone. When we act together *effectively*, it can be a geometric increase in what we do singly. In our engagement and openness to hear and learn, we enrich ourselves not only in learning about others, including those with whom our lack of understanding had long bred mistrust and alienation, but, paradoxically, when we must explain clearly our own traditions to others and test our long-held assumptions by the new perspectives we encounter in our exchanges with others, we deepen and sharpen our understanding of our own faith traditions.

In the struggle for religious freedom, this has built deeper knowledge and understanding of faiths that may be facing discrimination or persecution and stronger collegiality to stand up for each other when any groups face governmental or societal oppression. And in the very act of meeting and sharing and dialoguing and working together to bridge the divides and enhance the cooperation, we are modeling of the kind of world of which we dream and which we strive to create.

I have long wrestled with Michael Sandel's formulation of claims of religious conscience vs claims of religious choice. Sandel's early writings on religious liberty provide a central theme for Freeman's essay. Conscience, according to Sandel, and I believe Freeman concurs in this, comes from a recognition of the moral, cultural, and social ties and responsibilities that bind communities—including religious communities—together and induce compelled or commanded behaviours, rather than choices. The focus on exercising choice is derived, according to Sandel and Freeman, from a rights-oriented approach to law and politics most indicative of the human rights structures of most contemporary democratic nations. This gives total autonomy to the individual, so that rights are understood to be exercised always as a function of choice. As I said above, and have offered illustrations (circumcision, eating kosher or halal food for Jews and Muslims), I agree that conscience claims are often harder for non-believers to understand and appreciate, and it is therefore harder to craft laws and policies that protect the religious freedom rights involved.

My concerns with Sandel's formulations fall along several lines.

First, the difference between the conscience claims and choice claims is not always clear. Is going to worship services a matter of compelled conscience or choice? On one level, is the decision whether or not to eat kosher food, truly something over which a Jew has no choice? If, as a matter of faith, Jews believe they have a covenantal relation with God, who has commanded them to eat kosher foods, you have no real choice. On another level, however, you make a choice every time you sit down to eat. Indeed, at a deeper level, you have already made the choice whether to be bound by the covenant. Whatever it is outside ourselves with which we are encumbered, and which imposes responsibilities on us, we chose to be encumbered by it. Several times, Freeman acknowledges the difficulty of drawing this line (as in his discussion of Aboriginal sacred land rights and LGBTQ rights, which he suggests take a similar form to religious freedom claims). But more expansively than the examples he raises, I would argue that almost anything that one person sees as clearly a choice, another might sincerely frame as being motivated by conscience. Should the two people standing before a court arguing for religious freedom protections on these differing grounds be treated differently?

Exactly why should a right, which feels compelled as a matter of faith, be any more or less protected than other expressions of religious freedom because the latter contain elements of choice? Where Sandel in his foundational essay on the subject, "Religious

Liberty—Freedom of Conscience or Freedom of Choice",[28] gives no examples of claims that fall on one side or the other, focusing instead on characterizing several prior United States Supreme Court cases, in other writings, he gives examples of choosing to feed your children before other children, caring for your mother before other mothers, and bombing your own town as an air force pilot commanded to do so. But these were not intended to exemplify his basic claim about religious liberty. Freeman does offer interesting examples of the differences between choice and conscience. Advocating a nativity scene being placed on public property is offered as an example of choice. But one could frame the need to bring the 'good news' of the birth of their saviour to the public on public space designated for important displays as a matter of conscience. Should a conscience-claim version of this be given more weight than a rights version? Further, would a nativity display be any more or less protected than a church community arguing that they have a conscience belief that they must run a program for homeless or hungry people, despite zoning laws to the contrary, or provide sanctuary to a non-documented immigrant fleeing religious (or other) persecution?*

---

* For a court's assessment of what constitutes a legitimate conscience claim for an individual, whose views should the court consider: the individual or the religious authorities of the faith group to which they belong? At least in United States law, the answer generally is the individual. Perhaps the real question at stake here is the sincerity of the religious claim. In that context, should a court differentiate between an individual making claims that flow from hierarchical denominations where the idea of an official position and a commanded sense of conscience are more self-evident? And is there a difference between more fundamentalist churches with a more dogmatic theology from liberal denominations?

In recent decades there has developed a tendency to associate more fundamentalist religious views as more authentic. There was a time in the middle of the 20th century when authentic religious voices were connected to the more moderate or "mainline" religious traditions: Rabbi Stephen S. Wise, Reverend John Haynes Homes, John Courtney Murray SJ, Reinhold Niebuhr, Pope John XXIII, and non-clerical public figures like Jinnah of Pakistan and Gandhi of India. Today there seems to be a popular equation of fundamentalism and authenticity. By definition, fundamentalist expressions of religion tend to play a more encompassing role in the lives of practitioners, making those binding ties that Sandel lifts up more self-evidently sincere than might seem claims derived from more liberal theological

Secondly, how should Sandel's distinctions lead us to think about the choice people make about which religion they wish to be a practitioner of? Is it not a 'human right' to change your beliefs? Religious freedom, as protected under Article 18 of the Universal Declaration of Human Rights and the ICCPR includes the right to choose and change one's religion. Indeed, even our most deeply held conscience beliefs and faith beliefs may be reshaped by exposure to reasoned discourse or to new spiritual experiences leading us to accept (or choose) new expressions of faith. From Augustine to Aquinas (*Summa Theolgica*) to John Paul II (*Fides et Ratio*), there is a long and treasured tradition in Catholicism, as there is in Judaism and Islam, which recognises the interaction between faith and reason and recognises the influence each can have on the other. Is not conscience itself a manifestation of existential choices we make including the influences we chose to allow ourselves to be encumbered by?

Thirdly, the assertion that "the failure of democratic leaders to [comprehend the worldview with which the encumbered person is connected,] results in Heydon's tyranny of relativism," raises troubling issues. There is no guarantee that the value system to which the encumbered person is connected is that represented by the common good or the good life as Sandel asserts. The families, communities, schools, societal institutions, and political institutions of dictatorial regimes—right-wing or communist— seek to inculcate the same "take it on faith" loyalty, obedience,

---

denominations where practitioners are more likely to have overlapping identities. For such liberal believers, these overlapping identities may raise questions as to what extent religion, as opposed to other sources, is the motivating factor and whether a claim made for religious conscience should be as readily accepted as sincere. While courts have some need to assess the sincerity of religious claims with legal consequences (claims of families creating their own church to enjoy special tax benefits; prisoners who make up new religions to claim special privileges) to have courts regularly evaluating the sincerity of religious claims being brought before them, would take democracies down a very dangerous path of judges sitting in judgment of what is in the heart of people and which religions can produce sincere conscience claims and which not.

and acceptance. Or in dealing with the racism, which Freeman discusses, against Australia's Aboriginal populations (or the racism found in so many times and climes that argued that Blacks or Jews were sub-human) they were also connected with value systems outside those who espoused such views and were nourished by those value systems including, too often, religious value systems.

Relatedly, as those who advocate for internationally recognised rights related to religious freedom know all too well, some countries are dominated by a specific faith group that is integrated in the governing structures. They claim that they should be free of restrictions from international accords because their family life, cultural norms, ethical views, and governing structures are tied to the one true religion. They assert a religious claim to justify their repression of divergent religious views. So too for non-religious countries like North Korea or China, who assert other values that bind their nations together in a manner that leaves no room for free exercise of religion (particularly those expressions of religion that might challenge their authority). Is it plausible that such countries or communities can find resonance in Sandel's conceptual view to justify their imposing on people their moral system outside the framework of internationally recognised human rights? In what way, under what standard, can we compellingly refute such a claim demonstrating that our sense of the common good and the good life is a more morally, legally, or even religiously legitimate measure than their religious, cultural, or political value system would impose? In this sense, is not the religious conscience approach to religious freedom as likely to result in moral relativism as the rights approach?[29]

So, I wonder how many readers believe, derived by reason or by intuitive sense, that rather than two different approaches to religious freedom in the world, each incomprehensible to the other; most of us are a mix of encumbered selves in some ways and unencumbered in others?*

Fourthly, Freeman's analysis has relevance to what is increasingly a momentous debate and difficult challenge in most democratic countries today: what happens when competing claims (whether of conscience or of fundamental rights) are in tension with each other? In particular, how should we balance religious freedom claims of conscience not to obey civil rights laws against the importance of such laws in protecting the fundamental rights of protected categories? There are those who argue that while each person has an absolute right to believe whatever their conscience dictates, when turned into action, religious freedom claims should not interfere with the state's compelling interest in civil rights laws. Often such proponents will argue that the burden on religious freedom from following civil rights laws is not substantial while the danger of endless numbers of people entitled to claim religious exemptions from such laws would undermine the entire structure of civil rights protections. Conversely, religious freedom proponents

---

* This approach, I would argue, resonates with the way that Judaism thinks about the role of choice behind every religious act we perform—or the approach of any faith that places free will at the centre of human existence. The Jewish tradition takes a paradoxical view on the issues Sandel raises. Jewish law is a system of commandments that stands outside of each Jew, that flowed from a covenant between God and the Jewish people at Sinai, who accepted the commandments in constructive agency for all the generations to come. As opposed to a rights-oriented worldview, all of traditional Jewish life is structured around duties, commandments, obligations that flowed from that covenant for each Jew who chooses to accept these obligations—exactly the kind of exercise of conscience Sandel and Freeman are concerned about. Indeed, there is no word for "rights" in classical Hebrew. Yet free choice is at the core of Judaism's normative philosophy. As the revered medieval philosopher Moses Maimonides wrote (Teshuvah 5:1-6):

> Free will is given to every human being. If we wish to incline ourselves toward goodness and righteousness, we are free to do so; and if we wish to incline ourselves to evil, we are also free to do that. From Scripture (Genesis 3:22) we learn that the human species, with its knowledge of good and evil, is unique among all earth's creatures. Of our own accord, by our own faculty of intelligence and understanding, we can distinguish between good and evil, doing as we choose. Nothing holds us back from making this choice between good and evil—the power is in our hand.

So, from a Jewish perspective, every day, every act involves an element of choice.

would argue that any time the state forces an individual to violate his religious conscience, it is a serious restriction of religious freedom and such exemptions should routinely be allowed. They argue that the burden on those protected by civil rights laws in seeking other landlords, employers, or public accommodation (stores, restaurants, hotels) who will not discriminate is not substantial. They might well argue that the inability of civil rights advocates to understand the consequence of a state forcing someone to violate their religious conscience is exactly the kind of incomprehensibility of which Freeman warns, and to which Sandel urges more sensitivity.

It is true that the hardest debates in a democracy are those that pit valid moral principles against each other. And that is the case here. Because both sides think they are right and some cannot see the valid claims on the other side of this vexing debate, there are those who want their side to 'win' this battle of competing rights. At the same time, there are some who can see validity on both sides and who seek to find common ground and compromise. Public opinion polls in most Western-style democracies on attitudes about reproductive rights and LGBTQ rights, suggest that the arc of history swings towards those civil rights claims, with the younger generation of even Evangelical and Catholic Christians being, for example, far more receptive to gay rights and gay marriage than their parents. Those attitudes are filtering increasingly into legislative bodies as elected officials become younger and for social conservatives that could be an incentive to seek some kind of compromise now. Courts, however, are not subject to public opinion polls and in the United States, for example, where there has been a significant shift to the right in the federal courts, with President Trump's far younger and more conservative appointments than either his Republican or Democratic predecessors made, there may be significant retrenchment in reproductive and LGBTQ rights. For social liberals, this might argue for keeping these issues out of the courts by seeking common ground or compromise.

There have been some successful efforts in this regard. One well-known effort was the so-called 'Utah compromise', where representatives of the Mormon church, which is dominant in that state, other religious leaders, gay rights and women's rights leaders were able to find compromise on a number of these issues. It remains to be seen if this will become a model for other states and nations.[30] My own view is that allowing blanket religious exemptions for civil rights laws risks shattering the entire schema of civil rights protections and the balance must tip towards ensuring civil rights. In contrast, within the constraints of ensuring there remain strong protections against discrimination in hiring, housing, education, and public accommodations, there are creative ways to accommodate some religious conscience claims that emerge (e.g. exemptions for small businesses, for landlords who live in a home where they let rooms to others, and for individual employees who have fellow employees who can seamlessly cover for them if they are asked to do things that violate their conscience). Already, in the United States, there are variants of such exemptions that are functioning. This is an area in which varied countries sharing their best practices can be of great value.

In the final part of his essay, Freeman turns primarily to Rabbi Jonathan Sacks, one of the most respected and influential Jewish—indeed, religious—public intellectuals of this generation. Freeman focused on insights he draws from Sacks's book, *The Dignity of Difference*. Rabbi Sacks does offer strong support for many of the core contentions in Freeman's general analysis of religious freedom and Freeman offers a clear and compelling presentation of Rabbi Sacks's thought. But continuing my concerns about Sandel's approach, I think Freeman misreads one crucial conclusion relevant to our earlier discussion of Professor Sandel when he asserts:

> Sacks does not hold out much hope that human rights discourse of the post-Second World War era will uphold the dignity of

difference because it succumbs to universalism. "It suggests that the particularities of a culture are mere accretions to our essential and indivisible humanity, instead of being the very substance of how most people learn what it is to be human."

I agree with Freeman and Sacks on this latter sentence if the universalism Sacks critiques is that which suggests that, if there are universal values, there must also be a common universal way in which these values are inculcated, passed on to the next generation, function as a source of social cohesion. Sacks argues that in every culture, nation, religion there are very particularist ways that such values are inculcated, validated, and used to bring people together. This idea has a long tradition, perhaps most influentially articulated in modern times by Emil Durkheim. But more anciently, it also resonated with the talmudic assertion of a Noahide Covenant conveying ethics for all humanity and a normative view in Judaism that there is more than one path to salvation: that any religion that recognises the one God and calls its adherents to living an ethical life can offer a path to salvation . . . a kind of proto-religious tolerance and freedom concept.

But Sacks's broader argument is not the condemnation of the structure of international human rights, which focusing on this one sentence suggests. Rather than rejecting this rights-oriented approach, Sacks praises it but points out its limitation. He argues simply that it isn't sufficient because it isn't clear as to how it deals with the dignity of difference—the recognition of the pluralistic, multiple, varied ways these rights that inure in human dignity are expressed, validated, and inculcated (exactly Freeman and Sandel's point). Sacks clarifies it is not 'either/or' but 'both/and' in the very discussion in *The Dignity of Difference* to which Freeman alludes:

After 1945, the world placed its faith—as did the French

Revolution—in a universal code of human rights. This is our contemporary equivalent of the biblical covenant with Noah . . ."[31] *There is much to be said for this, but it is only half of what is needed for the coexistence of diverse cultures.* No universal code as such tells us what we would lose were the multiplicity of civilizations to be reduced, were one culture to dominate all others, were distinctive voices to be lost from the conversation of mankind. The abstract language of rights fails to enter into the depth of what Hinduism means to a Hindu, or Confucianism mean to its devotees. (Emphasis added.)

As I am urging, Rabbi Sacks clearly acknowledges the validity of the two complementary dynamics—the schema of international human rights to protect the dignity and value of human life for all humanity, with obligations of all nations to protect those rights, even while recognising it must be complemented by honouring the varied ways that differing religions, cultures, and communities inculcate, validate, and implement those values. The latter, of course, reflect Sandel and Freeman's encumbered bonds through which those particularist connections forge believers' understanding of the common good or the good life and the commanding presence that shapes their conscience.

The bottom line is that contemporary forms of religious freedom should protect the free exercise of religion whether as a matter of conscience or choice. Freeman's warning that conscience claims are often harder for non-believers to understand and less likely to be defended, should galvanise all committed to religious freedom. But, conversely, all should affirm and act to protect the schema of international human rights, including religious freedom rights, so under attack today by growing authoritarian forces on the right and by those left-wing forces which suggest that such rights are not universal but a manifestation of Western cultural and legal imperialism being imposed on other countries. I see in Freeman and Turner's

weave together a more holistic sense of what religious freedom should mean in the twenty-first century.

7

Islamophobia and secularism in liberal democracies

Riaz Hassan

L IBERALISM, DEMOCRACY, SECULARISATION, liberty, individualism, the primacy of reason, and equality are among the enduring legacy of the Enlightenment. As well as influences that have made and shaped the modern world, they are also some of the topics discussed in the erudite essays by Bryan Turner and Damien Freeman. In this essay, I offer some observations on the liberal state, secularism, civil society, and Islamophobia.

Liberalism enshrined the ideas of democracy, protecting and enhancing individual liberty, secularism, periodic affirmation of the ruling classes by the people, the rule of law, civil and human rights, and equality before the law, and paved the way for the rise of the liberal state, market economy, and capitalism. It elevated reason and scientific evidence as the sole arbiter of knowledge about the physical and social worlds, thus laying the foundation for the Industrial Revolution.

These developments, however, took a circuitous route to fulfil their promise to the masses. Take the idea of democracy. The most famous version of "We, the People" was set down in the American Constitution. It states, "We, the people of the United States, in order to form a more perfect Union, establish Justice, insure domestic Tranquility, provide for the common defence, promote the general Welfare, and secure the Blessings of Liberty to ourselves and our Posterity, do ordain and establish this Constitution for the United States of America." This declaration now legitimises all modern states and is accepted as good. From it, the most benign forms of human rule have been devised.

The promise embedded in the above declaration, however, was extended only to some, not *all the people*. It was written by fifty-five middle-aged white gentlemen of the highest rank and property, who claimed to represent the people of thirteen colonies. Yet they did not include women, slaves, or Native Americans. In the Britain of the day, the people comprised groups of propertied men (gentlemen, merchants, manufacturers, and artisans) but not *the populace below*. They were recognised as citizens, but citizen rights were stratified. The populace had legal and civil rights but not political rights.[1]

In *Dark Side of Democracy,* sociologist Michael Mann argues that liberal democracies, through their stress on individualism, are beneficent because their constitutions first and foremost protect individual human rights. However, if the two meanings of "We the People" ("demos and ethnos")* are fused, problems arise for other ethnic groups living in the same territory. The privileges of citizenship may involve discrimination against ethnic out-groups, who may be excluded and cleansed from the territory of *the people*. Mann argues that in regions where the population is relatively homogeneous but stratified by class, the state's role is

---

* These are Latin words. I am presuming Mann means citizens vs ethnics/others.

to act as a mediator between the competing interests of classes and interest groups. In territories where people are conceived of as organic—as one indivisible ethnic group—purity is maintained by the suppression of religious and ethnic minorities and even cleansing. This, he argues, is the dark side of democracy and democratisation.[2]

The challenge of social and ethnic diversity was indeed embedded in the preamble of the American Constitution: "We, the People". The Constitution excluded Native Americans, people without property, and women. Their inclusion in the share of the promise of equality and liberty only came after a long struggle. By the eighteenth century, the majority of the liberal democratic states had colonised large parts of the world for capitalist exploitation and political and cultural domination.

Colonialism was a disgraceful robbery of land and resources from large segments of the human population to satisfy the incessant greed of the colonising imperial power. There is an African saying: "When white men came, we had the land and they had the Bible now we have the Bible and they have the land." The incorporation of colonies into the economies of the colonial powers destroyed indigenous economies and subjugated the natives and their cultures. Never before had so many societies and cultures been subjected to such oppressive and racist exploitation and humiliation.[3]

As Turner and Freeman show in their contributions, the separation of church and state—i.e. secularism—is a defining feature of liberal democracies. There is voluminous literature on the topic and on its centrality in democracy and modernity. In his book on the subject, American sociologist Jose Casanova points to three elements of secularism:[4]

a. the increasing structural and institutional differentiation of social spaces and functions, resulting in the separation of religion from politics, economy, science, law, and other institutions;

b. the privatisation of religion in its own space; and,

c. the declining social significance of religious beliefs, commitment, and institutions (the last of which receives much attention in Freeman's essay).

The worldwide ascendancy of politicised religion in modern and modernised societies has led many commentators to question the secularisation thesis and to ask whether it indicates a revolt against modernity and a failure of the modernisation process. Casanova saves the secularisation thesis by making it normative, arguing that for society to be modern it must be secular, and for it to be secular it must relegate religion to non-political spaces. The de-privatisation of religion, he argues, is not a refutation of the thesis if it occurs in ways that are consistent with the requirements of modern society and promote liberal values.[5] My research on Muslim societies shows that in societies where religion and politics are fused, religious institutions lose public trust, whereas they gain public trust when they are separated.

Sociologist Niklas Luhmann also offers a typology of the role of religion in modern society. He agrees that institutional differentiation and functional specialisation form distinctive features of modern society. They give rise to autonomous functional instrumentalities, such as polity, law, economy, science, education, health, art, family, and religion. One consequence of the increased institutional autonomy in modern societies is that major institutions have become independent of religious norms and values, a process Luhmann calls 'secularisation'. In such conditions, the degree of public influence that religion enjoys depends on how it relates to other institutions in society.

Luhmann uses the terms 'function' and 'performance' to analyse this relationship.

'Function', in this context, refers to 'pure' religious communication, variously called devotion and worship, the care of souls, or the search for salvation and enlightenment. Function is the pure, social communication which involves the transcendent, and the element that religious institutions claim for themselves on the basis of their autonomy in modern society. 'Religious performance', in contrast, occurs when religion is 'applied' to problems generated in other institutional systems but not solved there or simply not addressed anywhere else, such as economic poverty, corruption, political oppression and so on. Religious institutions gain public influence through the 'performance' role they play by addressing these non-religious or 'profane' problems.[6]

For Luhmann, the functional problem of religion in modern society is a performance problem. Religious institutions gain public influence when they efficiently carry out their performance role. This requires religious institutions to be autonomous *vis a vis* the state and other institutional subsystems. A logical deduction from this premise is that religious institutions will gain greater public influence in institutional configurations where they are autonomous from the state. If they are not, they cannot carry out their performance function effectively. This means religious institutions will enjoy, in theory, greater public influence in a differentiated, namely secular, state social formation, compared to in an undifferentiated state social formation. Luhmann's model was empirically supported by the findings of my work on Muslim societies.[7]

Luhmann's model also offers a framework that can be applied in empirical studies of secularisation and its correlates in modern states and societies. It can also be applied to ascertain the relative robustness of civil society. As British social philosopher Ernest Gellner has argued, the core of civil society is the idea of institutional and ideological pluralism, which has prevented the central institutions of the state from establishing a monopoly of power and truth in society.[8] He argues that robust civil society is essential for the growth and development of knowledge, science, and technology. This can only happen in a civil society which privileges *doubt and reason,* not *conviction and truth.* Secularism has contributed much to the existence of strong and vibrant civil societies in modern states. This is shown in the presence of leading universities in many modern states. In contrast, in many Muslim-majority countries, religious developments are not conducive to the development of a civil society based on doubt and reason. This may be one reason that universities in most Muslim countries do not rank high in global rankings.

Islamophobia denotes negative, hostile, and irrational attitudes towards Islam and Muslims. The term has gained wide currency in recent years, taking root in public, political, and academic discourses. Its recent popularity, however, belies the fact that the term has a long history in Western academic discourse. The notions surrounding the term have an even longer history. British scholar of Islamic studies Katherine Zebiri, for instance, notes that contemporary Islamophobia is nothing more than "the most recent manifestation of an age-old hostility to Islam on the part of Christendom and the West".[9]

Since at least the time of the Crusades, the 'West' has perpetuated a negative 'othering' discourse about Islam. The religion of Islam has been perceived as violent and perpetuated "by the sword", characterized by "perverted practices" and "essentially untrustworthy".[10] Like its contemporary manifestation, the discourse has been largely impervious to evidence or reason. Confrontations between the Muslim world and the West in more recent history—such as colonialism—have further served to cement negative perceptions of Muslims in the Western mind.[11] Colonial powers used an anti-Islam discourse to drive their project to civilise and enlighten the Muslim populations they had subdued. Key to this was positioning Islam (and Muslims) as irrational, barbaric, and backward.[12]

The term 'Islamophobia' has been evident in Western academic discourses for almost a century. The word is believed to have first emerged in its French form—*Islamophobie*—in 1922. Etienne Nasreddine Dinet, a French writer and painter, who spent significant time in Algeria, denoted an 'Islamophobe' as one who "makes incorrect generalisations about Muslims, misrepresents the religion of Islam or displays an unfounded hostility towards it". Dinet saw the phenomenon as either politically motivated or prompted by personal interests, and he vehemently denounced those who, from his point of view, only learnt Arabic and studied the Islamic religion for the purpose of disparaging it.[13]

Edward Said's book, *Orientalism*, affirms that the 'West' has long associated Islam with negative images, sentiments, and stereotypes.[14] Political theory privileges reason in the name of liberal principles so Islamic states are seen as non-secular and devoid of reason because of their proximity to religion. In the making of the nation state through secularism, religion becomes the problem and not Islam. Islam ends up becoming the religion which is the problem. Consequently, Islamophobia emerges as a phobia of religion in the secular state. This phobia dominates anti-Muslim sentiments in Western secular democracies where Muslims are discriminated against for being Muslim, even when they are citizens of the nation state.[15]

More recently, the term Islamophobia has come to refer to "unfounded hostility towards Islam, and thus fear or dislike of all or most Muslims".[16] Its place was confirmed in contemporary discourses by the publication of the well cited report *Islamophobia: A Challenge For Us all*, published by a British think-tank, the Runnymede Trust.[17] Since then it has been used by political activists, nongovernmental organizations, public commentators, and international organizations to draw attention to harmful rhetoric and actions directed at Islam and Muslims in Western liberal democracies, and to denounce such sentiments.

The Runnymede report describes Islamophobia as a useful shorthand way of referring to dread or hatred of Islam and unfounded prejudice and hostility towards Islam and Muslims that, by implication, translates into "fear or dislike of all or most Muslims". In determining what kinds of attitudes or speech constitute Islamophobia, the report differentiates between "narrow" and "open" views of Islam. Open views are those that can be considered legitimate criticism of Islam, while narrow or "closed" views are those that constitute Islamophobia. The report identifies eight "closed" views that are typical of the phenomenon:

- Islam is perceived as "monolithic and static": all Muslims are alike, believe the same things, and hold the same worldview.
- Islam has nothing in common with other religions in terms of values. It is "separate and 'other'".
- Muslims are "inferior": they are uncivilised, unenlightened, and hold outdated views about women and the modern world.
- Islam is, essentially, "hostile, violent and aggressive". It is the "enemy" of the West.
- Muslims are "devious" and "manipulative", looking for "strategic military or political advantage".
- It is justifiable to discriminate against Muslims.
- Muslims' criticism of the West should not be paid heed to, but it is justifiable to criticise Islam or Muslims.
- It is "normal" and "natural" to be prejudiced against Muslims. This is not a form of bigotry.

The report goes on to discuss the practical consequences of such hostility towards Muslims, including unfair discrimination against Muslim individuals and communities and the exclusion of Muslims from mainstream political and social affairs.

The Runnymede report provided a significant benchmark in the discourse on Islamophobia. Its definition is still one of the most frequently referred to in discussions about anti-Muslim sentiments. It also served to stimulate further study of the phenomenon.

Since 1997, many scholars have used the formulation of the Runnymede Trust in their conceptualisations of Islamophobia as a "fear and dread of Islam",[18] "a social anxiety towards Muslim cultures" and a "fear of Muslims and [the] Islamic faith".[19] Islamophobia has been described as a "rejection of Islam, Muslim groups and Muslim individuals on the basis of prejudice and stereotypes".[20] For example, Schwartz,[21] director of the Center for Islamic Pluralism, elaborates that Islamophobia involves the "condemnation of Islam in its entirety as 'extremist'", which, by its very definition, fails to acknowledge the majority of Muslims who do not take extremist positions.

Other authors liken Islamophobia to other discriminative discourses, such as xenophobia and racism, which are similarly characterized by fear and prejudice. Australian social scientists Poynting and Mason noted that Islamophobia evolved from "anti-Asian and anti-Arab racism" to target Muslims in particular.[22] Perhaps what unites the definitions is the widespread acknowledgment that Islamophobia is, indeed, "a social evil" and a core element of the phenomenon is the emotion of fear.

A comprehensive analysis of Islamophobia was presented several years later by American political scientist Erik Bleich in his 2011 paper published in the *American Behavioral Scientist* journal, entitled "What is Islamophobia, and How Much is There? Theorizing and Measuring an Emerging Comparative Concept".

Bleich defines Islamophobia as "indiscriminate negative attitudes or emotions directed at Islam or Muslims".[23]

Like the Runnymede report, Bleich acknowledges that not all negative attitudes or emotions directed towards Islam or Muslims constitute Islamophobia. However, Bleich argues that Islamophobia is not "an all-or-nothing proposition". It cannot be seen simply as an "open" or "closed" view. Instead, it is likely to be more "graded". For example, a one-off negative opinion about Islam or Muslims will constitute low-level Islamophobia, especially if the opinions can be revised or altered based on new information. At the other extreme, expressions of persistent unshakable hostility are high-level Islamophobia. The more consistently an individual expresses a great number of such intensely held biases, the more Islamophobic he or she is. The greater the prevalence, consistency, and intensity of Islamophobic expressions and individuals, the greater the Islamophobia in a given social group or society.

In 2017, the Runnymede Trust released a new report on the phenomenon: *Islamophobia—Still a Challenge For Us All.*[24] Against the backdrop of increasing anti-Muslim hate crimes in Britain, the report conceded that Islamophobia had become more complex and entrenched in recent years. It acknowledged that much of the public debate surrounding Islamophobia lacked appropriate "nuance", and that while its earlier definition of Islamophobia was an appropriate mechanism for encouraging accountability, a new definition of Islamophobia was needed. It therefore proposed that Islamophobia be defined as:

> any distinction, exclusion, or restriction towards, or preference against, Muslims (or those perceived to be Muslims) that has the purpose or effect of nullifying or impairing the recognition, enjoyment or exercise, on an equal footing, of human rights and fundamental freedoms in the political, economic, social, cultural

or any other field of public life.

Notably, the Trust's new definition clearly positions Islamophobia as akin to a form of racism. Like racism, the phenomenon is not simply a range of negative attitudes but has practical ramifications, "denying people dignity, rights and liberties across a range of political, economic, social and cultural institutions". It is the widespread structural inequalities and extensive disadvantages that Islamophobia presents for Muslims that the Runnymede Trust attempts to capture in this definition.

Other authors have also reached the conclusion that attitudes akin to 'racism' are an intrinsic part of Islamophobia. Australian social scientists led by Kevin Dunn note that Islamophobia shares many elements in common with contemporary forms of racism because it depicts Muslims as 'others', characterized by "incivility, inferiority and incompatibility".[25] American legal scholar Khaled Beydoun, argues that the "racial framing of Muslim identity . . . not only converges with the rising tide of anti-Muslim animus . . . but indeed [is] an integral part of it".[26] Other authors have termed Islamophobia as a form of cultural racism: where the hatred and hostility of others [is] based on religious beliefs, cultural traditions, and ethnicity. Instead of animosity stemming from racial identity, it is expressed "in terms of cultural and religious inferiority".[27]

While the term 'Islamophobia' has cemented its place in contemporary discourses about anti-Muslim sentiments, the term itself has come under criticism in academic and broader circles. Some authors reject the term because they argue it stifles freedom of expression and people's right to raise legitimate concerns about Islamic beliefs and practices. Other authors have expressed reservations about the word because of its reference to *phobia*, which implies that "the object of fear is Islam as a religion".[28] For these authors, phobia is a misnomer because it suggests "a mental illness or a fear", rather than a form of prejudice. British sociologist Fred Halliday, a prominent protagonist of this view, argues that Islam is no longer the foe. It is no longer "threatening to win large segments of western European society to its faith, as Communism did, nor is the polemic, in press, media or political statement, against the Islamic faith... The attack now is against not *Islam* as a faith but *Muslims* as a people". He argues that the term should be replaced with 'Muslimophobia' in its stead.[29] Despite these concerns and criticisms, no other term has yet managed to gain the level of acceptance that Islamophobia has. While it may have some shortcomings, the term continues to provide a useful starting point for studies and discussions of negative attitudes and views about Islam and Muslims.

The term 'Islamophobia' has now been adopted by various international organizations, including the United Nations. Since 2004, various initiatives and reports have publicly condemned the phenomenon, lamenting its negative impact on Muslims. The European Commission against Racism and Intolerance, also examines the phenomenon of Islamophobia in the annual report on its activities. Its 2016 report expresses alarm that fear and hostility against Islam has become such a common phenomenon that "anti-Muslim arguments are . . . now also embraced by some mainstream politicians resulting in [a] growing xenophobic populist discourse". Yet despite the growing concern expressed by European intergovernmental bodies, it appears that the extent of the problem of Islamophobia in Europe is not well known. Such incidents tend to be "severely . . . under-documented in the EU" by its member states.[30]

In the United States, opinion polls reveal that almost 50% of Americans hold a negative view of Islam;[31] people generally associate negative words with Islam, including words associated with violence and terrorism;[32] and the majority of Americans are concerned about Islamic extremism. More recent studies suggest that the phenomenon of Islamophobia in America is increasing, evident from anti-Muslim bias and the number of hate crimes targeting Muslims.

Research on the extent of anti-Muslim sentiments in Australia has given a somewhat mixed picture to date. While Australian sociologist Gary Bouma, for instance, suggests that "inclusion is [still] the dominant discourse in Australia",[33] other authors argue that the presence of Muslims in Australia is increasingly being questioned.[34] In part, this last Australian political scientist's perspective reflects the ongoing historical presence of an anti-Muslim discourse,[35] although it appears that anti-Muslim and anti-Islam sentiments have been expressed with "greater intensity" in the past few years.[36]

Over approximately two decades, various studies have sought to examine Australians' attitudes towards Muslims. According to Australian political scientist Miller, opinion polls have revealed social distance*   between Muslim Australians and the broader population since the 1980s.[37] Likewise, polls conducted in the early 2000s found that a minority of Australians perceived Muslims to be a military or cultural threat to Australia.[38] In 2001, a University of New South Wales and Macquarie University survey found that "white Australians would be more concerned about a relative marrying a Muslim than any other minority",[39] while a 2007 study found that more than 17% of survey participants did not want Muslims in Australia.[40] A 2016 study conducted by Deakin University found that 60% of its participants would not be comfortable if a relative married a Muslim, while almost half of the participants did not disagree with "Islamophobic statements" such as "practising Muslims pose a threat to Australian society".[41]

---

*   Social distance here refers to the sociological concept of the degree of personal intimacy.

Other studies have revealed Muslims experiencing various forms of discrimination in Australia. A 2011 report by the Australian Human Rights Commission documented the negative reactions that Australian Muslim women face when wearing a veil (*hijab*) in employment or educational contexts, as well as hostile reactions from members of the public.[42] Australian economists Booth, Leigh, and Varganova's 2012 study also found that people with Middle Eastern names were more likely to experience discrimination when applying for employment.[43] Research conducted in 2015 found that Muslims living in Sydney were subject to a much higher rate of discrimination compared to other Australians.[44] Results from a 2017 study conducted by the Centre for Islamic Studies and Civilisation and Charles Sturt University indicated that Muslim women were three times as likely to face harassment when out in public, including physical assault.[45]

One particular source of data on attitudes towards Muslims in Australia is the Scanlon Foundation's Mapping Social Cohesion surveys, which have been conducted in conjunction with Monash University for the past decade.[46] The survey is the largest of its kind, with the most recent involving 42,000 participants. The 2016 report found that almost one quarter of Australians have "negative feelings about Muslims".[47] The 2017 report found that "strong negative views" towards Muslims remain prevalent and, in fact, had increased since the previous year's report.[48] What has been described as "new racism" sees Muslims as "threats to 'social cohesion' and 'national unity'" and to the "cultural values and integrity of the dominant (Anglo-Celtic) 'host' society".

A survey by the International Centre for Muslim and non-Muslim Understanding at the University of South Australia shows that while one in ten Australians display strong feelings of Islamophobia, the overwhelming majority don't share these feelings. This was true irrespective of where they lived, except in Victoria, where people were less likely to be Islamophobic. Islamophobic attitudes and feelings were strongly connected to low educational attainment, unemployment, and age. They were also correlated with non-traditional Christian groups, people from non-English speaking backgrounds, and anti-immigration views. Labor party supporters were significantly less Islamophobic, as were people who had contact with Muslims.[49]

Are negative attitudes towards Muslims becoming more common in Australia? Some commentators suggest that prejudice towards Muslims is only the latest manifestation of racism in a country that has a long history of such attitudes.[50] Others argue that the media has played a major role in fostering Islamophobic sentiments and that events overseas, such as terrorist attacks and the rise of the Islamic State and the violent atrocities it has committed, have tainted the perception Australians have towards all Muslims. Other scholars believe that Australia's political environment has allowed Islamophobia to take root by deliberately taking a step back from multiculturalism,[51] or by politicians either failing to take a public stance against Islamophobia or by explicitly making anti-Islam statements themselves. Political parties with anti-Islam platforms have also appeared in recent years, including One Nation and the Australian Liberty Alliance, which has allowed the Islamophobic discourse to become an overt part of Australian political discussions, yet without serious scrutiny or nuanced analysis.

In these brief concluding comments on the challenges facing the faith and believers and non-believers in the twenty-first century, I will focus on three factors: literacy, globalisation, and demography.

For much of human history, literacy was the prerogative of the clergy and ruling elites. However, this changed in modern Western societies during the last two centuries. The same is now happening in the rest of the world. Increasing literacy has important cognitive and sociological ramifications for the reproduction of social life. In his seminal studies, British social anthropologist Jack Goody has shown that in a non-literate society, cultural traditions are reproduced through a continuous series of interlocking face-to-face conversations in which the very conditions of reproduction operate in favour of consistency between the past and present.[52] This makes criticism—the articulation of inconsistency—less likely to occur. If it does, the inconsistency makes a lesser impact, and is more easily adjusted to or forgotten. Criticism in a non-literate society is personal and non-cumulative. It does not lead to a deliberate rejection and reinterpretation of social dogma, so much as to a semi-automatic readjustment of belief.

In literate societies, interlocking conversations go on but they are no longer the only medium of dialogue. Writing and reading provide alternative sources for the transmission of cultural orientations and they also favour awareness of inconsistency. One aspect of this is a sense of change and of cultural lag; another is the notion that cultural inheritance as a whole is composed of two very different kinds of material: on the one hand fiction, error, and superstition; on the other, elements of truth that can provide the basis for a more reliable and coherent explanation of the divine, human past, and the physical world. As the world's population becomes increasingly more literate, this will have significant implications for religion and for believers. It may heighten orthodoxy and freedom from it.[53] Religious switching trends in the world's most literate countries can be used as a proxy for these developments and trends.[54] At the time of writing, the High Court of Australia had quashed the conviction of Cardinal George Pell for child sex abuse, which he had vehemently denied. The case received wide media coverage and debate. Is it plausible that the scale of criticism and scepticism surrounding the case could happen only in a highly literate society like Australia?

Development of modern communication technologies has effectively removed barriers to communication and transformed the world into a global village; a 'single place'. A major sociological consequence of globalisation is that it has accentuated trends towards hybridity as well as orthodoxy. This has generated conflict between religious hybridity and authenticity, manifested across all religious communities. This will have major consequences for faiths and the faithful in the modern world, as well as for managing religious diversity.[55]

Demography of the world's religions will change markedly in the twenty-first century, with significant global consequences. Since Muslims have the highest fertility rate and the youngest average age, their population is projected to increase from 1.6 billion or 23% of the world's total population in 2010 to 2.76 billion or 30% by 2050. For the first time in history, Muslims will nearly equal Christians, who have been until now the world's largest religious group in size. If we take a longer-term view, by 2070, Islam will be the largest religion in the world, accounting for 35% of the world's population, compared to Christians, making up 34%.[56]

These changes will have significant repercussions for inter-religious relations around the world. Most modern countries have religious minorities. A recent study of minority status and socio-economic wellbeing showed that in India, which has the world's largest Hindu population and largest Muslim minority population, as the size of the Muslim population increases in a district, their wellbeing significantly declines.[57] The findings of another study on trust, ethnicity, and religion revealed that religious and ethnic affiliations appear to have a complex impact on social trust. Majority communities tend to consider minorities less trustworthy, yet minority religious communities tend to be more trusting of the majority.[58] If these findings hold globally, they will have significant sociological implications for inter-religious harmony. Sociological studies show that minorities' experience of relative depravation can lead to movements for social change, which rarely happens peacefully. Given that the twenty-first century will see countries becoming increasingly religiously diverse, there will be a pressing need for further consideration of how to develop appropriate public policies to manage religious and ethnic diversity and to promote inter-religious harmony. The success or failure of such policies will have important ramifications for the security and equality of believers, non-believers, and religions.

8

Incomprehension of religion in Australian society

James Franklin

TURNER AND FREEMAN raise many issues concerned with civil society, religion, and the relationship between them. This essay concentrates on just one of the most basic ones, raised especially by Damien Freeman. It is the growing ignorance of traditional religion, especially Christianity, in Australia.

Freeman rightly lays out the core commitments of religion, which threaten to become incomprehensible in the near future, especially to the 'educated'. They are: that there is something that transcends the material; that ethics and meaning are dependent on metaphysics (hence to be discovered, not constructed) and include some absolute obligations; and that institutions such as churches can help connect us to the transcendent.

Roy Williams's book, *In God They Trust?*,[1] describes how Australian prime ministers have, without exception, understood that. Nearly all were Christians (of a tolerant and not very sectarian variety), while even the non-religious ones, such as Gough Whitlam and Julia Gillard, had a good understanding of religion in their upbringing and an attitude similar to Clement Attlee's "Believe in the ethics of Christianity. Can't believe the mumbo jumbo."[2] Prime ministers are just an example. Until only yesterday, most people had a general idea of what religion was about and how religious people saw it bearing on ethics and public policy.

Now they don't. A secular mindset has grown up that instantiates not just hostility to religion but an unteachable incomprehension of it. Its most visible recent expression was the worldwide Handmaid's Tale protests of 2019, where protesters dressed in the style of the oppressed women of the TV series.[3] The point of the garb was to suggest that opposition to abortion stemmed from mindless theocracy.

The protests represent religion as an imposition of irrationally believed (alleged) arbitrary divine commands on peace-loving Enlightened folk who just want to be left alone. The incomprehension is led by philosophers, who of all people should have some subtlety in their understanding of ethical views. Probably the leader in the field of philosophical 'new atheism' is A. C. Grayling, who writes:

> It is time to refuse to tiptoe around people who claim respect, consideration, special treatment, or any other kind of immunity, on the grounds that they have a religious faith, as if having faith were a privilege-endowing virtue, as if it were noble to believe in unsupported claims and ancient superstitions.[4]

The same claims appear in a document that makes clear what consequences are to be drawn for imposing constraints on real people, the Brocher "Consensus statement on conscientious objection in healthcare".[5] It was issued by a group of fifteen philosophers and bioethicists in 2016, including leading Australian bioethicists Julian Savulescu, editor of the *Journal of Medical Ethics*, Jeanette Kennett, then president of the Australasian Association of Philosophy, and Justin Oakley, for many years director of Monash University's Centre for Human Bioethics. The essence of the document's position is contained in its opening paragraph:

> Healthcare practitioners' primary obligations are towards their patients, not towards their own personal conscience. When the patient's wellbeing (or best interest, or health) is at stake, healthcare practitioners' professional obligations should normally take priority over their personal moral or religious views.

The document speaks, like Grayling, as if faith in an unsupported superstition causes an opposition between "personal conscience" and the voice of reason, which speaks in favour of "patients' interests". That grossly misrepresents what doctors who conscientiously object to abortion and euthanasia are saying. They take a different view of what is in the patient's best interest, and they do so for publicly available reasons which are not just religious dogmas. Like any doctors, they are motivated by a desire to help their patients. They believe that the procedures they refuse to perform are destructive of the patients' interests, sometimes destructive of the patients themselves. So they refuse to perform those operations. To describe their concerns for patients as mere "personal moral or religious views" is wilfully to misunderstand their motivations.

Everyone knows—or did before the present outbreak of elected ignorance about religion—who the objectors mostly are. They are Catholics and other Christians who rely on a developed natural law philosophy of the intrinsic and irreducible worth of persons. That is a debatable philosophy, but it is not just a 'personal' belief. It has been defended publicly at length for centuries.[6]

It has to be admitted that philosophers of ill will (and non-philosophers of ill will, like Richard Dawkins and Christopher Hitchens) are not the only source of the present surge in ignorance of the Christian position on ethics. Just as philosophers should be in the lead with some subtlety of thought on foundational questions, but aren't, historians should be giving a comprehensive view of the thought-worlds of the past, but aren't. Although there is some excellent work on the religious history of Australia, such as Patrick O'Farrell's books on Catholics, Stuart Piggin and Robert Linder's recent *The Fountain of Public Prosperity: Evangelical Christians in Australian History*,[7] and Wayne Hudson's *Australian Religious Thought*,[8] the topic has remained a sectional interest. The mainstream of Australian historiography (except for Manning Clark) has been and remains a religion-free zone. It is dominated by a narrative according to which Australians since the noble founding convicts have been inspired by ideas such as imperialism, socialism, mateship, racism, nationalism, environmentalism, 'social justice', and money, but not religion.

That blindness is being reinforced by the current Australian history curriculum for schools. In the world history that occupies Year 8, the last historical figure identified as Christian is Charlemagne,[9] while the next two years' work on modern and Australian history simply writes religion out of the story (except for a tiny Year 10 module on 'Christians in contemporary Australia'). Meanwhile, the section on ethics in the curriculum bends over backwards to avoid mentioning the role that religion or any other metaphysical foundation might play in developing 'values'.[10] Australian historians and educational designers, not necessarily motivated by any explicit anti-Christian agenda, are engaged in cutting off present and future generations from knowledge of the religious motivations that have driven the past.

That is a human rights abuse perpetrated on children. John Finnis, the distinguished Australian philosopher of ethics and Oxford professor of law, summarises the aspects of human nature that are especially relevant to ethics in a list of what, he says, are self-evidently "basic aspects of my well-being", or "the basic forms of good for us": life (including health), knowledge, play, aesthetic experience, friendship, practical reasonableness, and religion.[11] He argues that they are all highly important, and incommensurable. To deprive children of access to any of them, say of knowledge, is a violation of their right to the opportunity to live a full human life. That applies as much to religion as to any other good in the list. It is a severe deprivation for someone if, in the crises of life, they have no conception of the spiritual side of reality, which might offer consolation and resources for resilience. But that is exactly what the present designed ignorance of religion accomplishes. Freedom from irreligion is as much needed as freedom of religion (and freedom from religion, in the sense of freedom from imposition of theocratic agendas).[12]

Then again, communication takes two. Australian Christians might also consider looking at the beam in their own eye when accounting for the failure of others to grasp the Christian view of ethics. The idea that ethics is based on (divinely created) human nature rather than directly on arbitrary divine commands is not exactly a common theme in sermons, catechisms, or religious literature. Even Catholicism, the denomination most committed to natural law theory, has not promoted the theory vigorously, not even in the comparatively user-friendly area of political and economic thought. Catholic social thought, based on the 1891 encyclical, *Rerum Novarum,* is an easy-to-understand theory, neither capitalist nor socialist, about how society is a natural cooperative ordering of special-purpose groupings, such as families, businesses, and unions. It has had enthusiasts in Australia, as recounted in Race Mathews's *Distributism in Victoria*,[13] but it is widely unknown in Catholic schools and pews. When the future prime minister, James Scullin, asked his parish priest what *Rerum Novarum* was about, he had no idea,[14] and things have not improved in the century since. It is not surprising if Catholics do not understand their church's views on comparatively more abstruse questions like bioethics. An organization with a theory needs to explain it to the troops on the ground, in catechism style or some modern equivalent.

Protestantism has lagged somewhat behind Catholicism in philosophical theory of ethics, having inherited from the Reformers a suspicion of fallen human reason and of 'nature' in Catholic natural law theory. But recent Protestant philosophers have advanced a serious foundational theory of ethics which is called a divine command theory but lacks the offensive 'discretion thesis' (that God could command bad acts to be good). It is more a divine resemblance theory, holding that what is good for us flows from the necessarily good nature of God.[15] That general line of thinking is adequate as a way of connecting our ethics to the transcendent so as to support the objectivity of ethics.

Needless to say, communication of the ethical message of Christianity has not been helped by the fact that for those without any particular contact with churches, most of what they know comes from headlines about sexual abuse. Churches cannot blame anyone else for that.

Roy Williams, in his book on the decline of religion in Australia, *Post-God Nation?*, calls attention to another factor responsible for the younger generation's assumption that religion is not worth thinking about. It is prosperity, especially in regard to health.[16] In earlier times, death and disease were omnipresent and every child knew the real threat of them. Serious questions about life and death were pressing. Now, the children's dentistry of the 1950s is a thing of the past, life-threatening disease in children is rare, and although the death rate still stands at what it always was, exactly one per person, death is hidden in nursing homes and palliative care wards. In the low-anxiety world of food, drink, and comfy sofas, as Freeman quotes Blackadder, there is no need to worry about death and medical catastrophe for the foreseeable future—until one is old and one's ideas on the big questions (or lack of ideas) are set in concrete. The aphorism, "There are no atheists in foxholes", suggests its converse, that if there are no foxholes then atheism will run rampant.

The outcome of letting ethical sensibilities float free from any religious or metaphysical foundation can be predicted by abstract deduction or observed by looking around at the actual results. The word 'woke' is exactly right, suggesting as it does a sudden awakening from ethical somnolence and grabbing for the nearest simplistic pretext for righteous indignation. Commitments to ethically shallow virtues like 'tolerance' and to ethically partial causes like 'environmentalism' will take the place of deeper virtues and causes (such as the virtue of humility and the cause of preventing foetal alcohol syndrome). Outbreaks of moral vanity, like statue-toppling mobs and tearful apologies for other people's actions, will take the place of serious thought about effective policies to improve the lot of people in difficult circumstances. Deplatformings and witchhunts will come to the fore, effective altruism and presumptions of innocence will move to the rear.

As Freeman cites Fukuyama, any relativism—understood as ethics free of a metaphysical base—"must ultimately end up undermining democratic and tolerant values". We can expect more of the same.

That is, we can expect more of the same actions that *tend* to undermine democratic values. Whether they actually will undermine them is much harder to predict. The reason is that democratic elections, especially with compulsory voting, are not determined by who feels most enraged and shouts loudest but by who gets the centrist swinging voters over the line. If quantity of rage had counted in 1975, Whitlam would have won in a landslide, but that is not how democracy works. The left expected victory for Remain, Hillary Clinton, and Bill Shorten—by no means radical propositions, any of them—but the polls were mistaken. The last two of those had religious aspects. Clinton represented the Obama-era healthcare policy that pitted the administration against the Little Sisters of the Poor in the Supreme Court,[17] while Trump, though no model Christian, appealed to some Evangelical and Catholic demographics. In the 2019 Australian election, Scott Morrison allowed himself to be photographed praying at church, then Rugby Australia chose to remind the electorate of the bully-boy aspects of leftism on the afternoon before the election by sacking its leading player for his statements on gays and hell. While almost no-one agreed with Israel Folau's non-standard religious views, the unexpected election result in rugby-playing States suggested that the decision had influenced sections of the electorate that rarely took an interest in politics.[18] More recently, the electoral impact of the massive Black Lives Matter outpouring of activism was tested in the Eden-Monaro by-election. The result was a rare swing to a sitting (conservative) government. In all recent elections, the main party representing wokist leftism, the Greens, has failed to make headway, though success has been hourly expected. While none of the evidence is conclusive, it would appear on balance that the crucial median voters, however ignorant of religion they may be, have no appetite for the persecutory measures sought by the far left. If they take a live and let live attitude to gay marriage, they take the same to religion. We are certainly "moving into a period of incivility" in the public square, as Bryan Turner writes, but away from the shouting, in the electoral 'ballast' of centrist voters that determine elections, who keep only half an eye on politics while going about their lawful affairs, there remains a strong commitment to the sort of tolerance that is shocked by 'cancel culture'. Even the massive public funding of Catholic education and health services, which is quite exceptional on a world scale, seems to be under no immediate threat—on the well-established principle of Australian public largesse since Governor Bourke's Church Act of 1836, 'Some for you, some for me.' And while it is possible for the democratic will to be subverted by judicial and bureaucratic activism, some limit is placed on that by the retention of appointments to the highest court and departmental offices in political hands. Although the ABC, academia, and Qantas are not subject to any such political control, neither are they authorised to change much on the ground, outside themselves.

Democracy interacts with demographics too, with significant effects in the long term. As Turner mentions, Muslim fertility in Australia is higher than Christian, but it is also true that atheist fertility is lower, by enough to make a significant difference over a generation.[19] It is natural to believe also, though hard to prove, that among religious people the enthusiastic believers have more children.

The upshot is that alarmist conclusions from the observed decline in religious affiliation, understanding of religion, democratic civility, and civic-mindedness may be correct, but that is far from certain. Top-down attempts to change the way things are done could be met by the pushback of Darryl Kerrigan in *The Castle*: "Tell 'em they're dreamin'."

Of course, if the China crisis worsens and swamps every other issue, all bets are off.

Conclusion: Rethinking religion

in a secular world

M. A. Casey

THIS IS THE WAY things were meant to go. Religion would gradually disappear from the world, lingering for a while only in the private lives of a declining minority. A generalised absence of religious longing or interest would slowly supplant deeply embedded habits of mind and heart, which looked beyond this world for sources of meaning, morality, and community. The religious defaults which had for centuries so powerfully determined the value of things—life, suffering, justice, virtue, work, wealth and poverty, family and sexuality, men and women—would be reset by the inexorable growth of knowledge and rationality.

Vain and self-defeating religious ideas of fulfilment based on sacrifice, endurance, and transcendence would be superseded by more realistic and humane ideas of flourishing, centred on the glories of human achievement and the boundlessness of possibility for the knowing, seeing, creative individual. The divisions and conflicts which religion caused directly or helped to sustain by legitimising separations and exclusions between human beings would be overcome by continually expanding the scope of being and experience which 'the human' can encompass. The hierarchies that religion sustained—of knowledge and value, of rights and status—would be broken down to create an empire of equality. The world would become at once more divergent and more homogenous, more diverse and more united, as experience became richer and more varied and as understanding converged on a deepening sense of shared humanity.

This vision of the end of religion postulates what the eminent sociologist of religion, José Casanova, describes as an "anthropocentric change in the conditions of belief", unfolding "as a process of maturation and growth, as a 'coming of age' and as progressive emancipation".[1] In this, it represents "the historical self-understanding of secularism", asserting "the superiority of our present modern secular outlook over supposedly earlier and therefore more primitive religious forms of understanding".[2] It also reflects what a former Archbishop of Canterbury, Rowan Williams, has described in a different context as "Enlightenment tribalism". This is the form of the secular which many take to be the "default setting" of modernity. "Westernising, 'technocratic', rights-oriented, and committed to individual autonomy as an ideal", it understands itself as a universally valid "rational norm for fully flourishing human existence".[3]

Casanova notes that in this understanding, "to be secular is to be modern, and therefore by implication to be religious means to be somehow not yet fully modern".[4] Williams also makes this point but describes its implications more explicitly: the "non-modern life is a deprived life", something "imperfectly human, so that life lived within these terms is less than it should be, less than the fullness that we now enjoy and have grown into". In this spirit, religion, as another instance of the non-modern, is "not just something other; it is something past. It does not belong now" and "its persistence is an anomaly". "In the prevailing mythology of modernity, what is normal is a particular kind of rationality which sees itself as universal—as opposed to the partial and unreasoning traditions that have been overthrown by enlightenment".[5]

It is an idea of progress based on a profound conviction about the secular not only as a more complete form of rationality, but as a higher civilisation. In this mythology, religion is not normal, not modern. It is something that is 'over', that does not belong now. Ways of life shaped by it are deprived and only imperfectly human. Those who have been emancipated from religious belief have attained a condition that sets them apart and above. There is no return to religion from here. "The very idea of going back to a surpassed condition" is "an unthinkable intellectual regression".[6]

What happens, however, if religion refuses to be over? The Pew Research Center's 2015 population projections on the future of the world religions strongly suggest that religious belief is not a condition likely to be surpassed any time this century. Global population is projected to increase by 35% to 9.3 billion in the decades between 2010 and 2050, which will increase the number of the religiously unaffiliated in the world ("atheists, agnostics and people who do not identify with any particular religion") by just under 100 million. As a share of world population, however, the unaffiliated will fall from 16.4 to 13.2%. Their increase in absolute numbers represents growth of 9% between 2010 and 2050, but the number of Muslims will increase by 73%, the number of Christians by 35%, and the number of Hindus by 34%.[7]

However these figures might be read, they make one thing clear: the world is becoming more religious, not less. Explanations can perhaps be offered along the lines (usually in more oblique language) that most of the world's population is more deprived, less human, less rational, and less modern than the populations of more secular places. If the repugnant nature of this sort of argument in principle is not sufficient reason to reject it, the complicated picture of rising living standards and rapid social and technological changes across the world at the very least places it under considerable doubt. A different response is required, working from a different perspective to that of the myth of universal secular destiny.

The point here is not to vindicate religious belief against theories of secularisation but to try to bring into sharper focus a reality which some in secular Western societies are reluctant to accept, and reluctant to contemplate at the level of their own fundamental assumptions. There may not be many willing to speak frankly of religion as something best understood as a stage in human development which we have outgrown and which others will eventually outgrow too, but the presuppositions that go with it—that religion is fundamentally irrational (or partly rational at best); that it is really only for those with lower levels of education or culture, for the emotionally and intellectually simpler; that religious people are mainly migrants (which is okay, to a point) or otherwise weird or suspect (which is not)—have a very long half-life. This is unlikely to change, because while most of the world will remain religious, secular societies are going to become more secular.[8] Australia is certainly on this trajectory as well.[9]

Casanova sees a future entailing "global humanity . . . becoming simultaneously more religious and more secular", and the religious and secular becoming more "intertwined".[10] A key characteristic of "the contemporary global moment is the fact that all forms of human religion, past and present, from the most 'primitive' to the most 'modern' are available for individual and collective appropriation". This calls into question "all teleological schemes of religious rationalization and development which tended to place 'primitive' and 'traditional' forms of religion as older human cultural forms to be superseded by more modern, secular, and rational ones".[11]

At the same time, the evidence from apparently irreversibly secularised societies such as East Germany "puts into question any notion of a general global desecularization", together with various socio-anthropological theories of human beings as inherently religious creatures ("homo religiousus"), and theories which highlight the indispensable function religion plays in "moral and social integration".[12] Different forms of secularism and different forms of resistance to it from religious communities mean that "how, where, and by whom the proper boundaries between the religious and secular ought to be drawn" are "hotly disputed and debated almost everywhere in the world today",[13] and likely to become more so in the years ahead. Navigating this situation from the purposes of public policy at home or foreign policy abroad will require much more engagement, generosity, and genuine curiosity about "the other", than the governing assumptions of superior secular civilisation allow.

This volume identifies two main problems that confront an increasingly secular society facing out into an increasingly religious world: the problem of blind spots, and the problem of incomprehension. One major blind spot is highlighted in Bryan Turner's essay. Over the last fifty years, people in Western societies have been watching—some with alarm, many with indifference—as levels of attendance, participation, and affiliation have slowly declined in the major Christian denominations. We have tended to assume, perhaps reflecting the personal experience of those who drifted away from some form of religious involvement earlier in life without their sense of morality and decency being adversely affected, that the decline of the churches and local parishes will not make all that much difference to how we live.

More recently, however, we have become alarmed at the way in which democratic life has fallen rapidly into disarray. Turner reminds us of the long tradition in political thought which "saw the solidarity of civil society and citizenship as the basis of a functional democracy", and draws attention to "individualistic and privatised forms of religion" which have grown as the adherence to the mainstream churches has broken down. Turner is concerned less with what the growth of "hybrid religiosity" and "individual spirituality" may mean for the future of religious life as such, than with what it means for democracy, citizenship, and solidarity. He sees this "religious individualism" as a form of secularisation "involving the loss of religious communalism as a basis of civil society". "If the churches have been among the main pillars of civil society," he writes, "then their decline must have negative consequence for civil life".

Turner also notes the impact that the decline of communal religious life has had (as one factor among many) on the transmission of the values on which democracy depends, including courtesy, respect for others, and decency. He comments, in particular, on the decline of civility among the elite and the political and cultural implications this has, evident in disregard for the concerns of ordinary people, the growing appeal of populism as a consequence, rising extremism on the left and the right, and the emergence at the margins of groups openly based on resentment such as Incels. "Declining civility spells out declining democracy".

Turner invokes civility in its customary meaning of "good manners and considerate behaviour", kindness towards the vulnerable, and respect for others, including "respect for difference". In her response to Turner's essay, Ursula Stephens picks up this point, noting how different Australian prime ministers have drawn on their own "religious beliefs and practices to model, encourage, enable, inspire, and challenge the nation" in a way which promotes civility and respect, in contrast to the more overtly political and divisive uses of religion that have featured in modern politics in recent decades. Stephens quotes Evgeniia Erenchinova and Elena Proudchenko to remind us starkly of what is at stake here, and the critical role religion and spiritual values have to play as "creative and constructive mechanisms working to stabilise the society [and] prevent its destruction".

To make the same point more mundanely, communal religion is one important source of humane and civil values on which democratic societies depend, and plays an important part in fostering a renewed commitment to them in successive generations. It does this less perhaps by expounding them (although this is indispensable) and more by putting them into practice, particularly in local communities. The parish-based branches of the Society of St Vincent de Paul are just one example. They put kindness, respect, and thoughtfulness for others into practice, not just through providing financial and material assistance (usually from locally raised funds), but also by simply visiting people: the old, the lonely, the sick, or those recovering from physical or mental illness; migrants and refugees; people just out of prison; parents, families, and individuals struggling with various hardships or on the way to recovering from them. The great strength of this model is people helping each other in their own local area, and doing so on the basis of a level of relationship between neighbours, rather than as a service provided by a remote central authority.

The work of voluntary organisations, including local religiously based organisations, is recognised and valued to a considerable extent in public policy and in public discussion. The relational dimension which religious service providers bring to their work, for example, is one reason for governments contracting welfare services to them (cheaper service delivery is another), and there is a high level of public support and admiration for the work of organisations like the Society of St Vincent de Paul and the Salvation Army (reflected in the affectionate nicknames they have been given—'Vinnies' and 'the Salvos'), among others. There are, however, important dimensions to the contribution that religious communities make which are significantly under-appreciated.

Some of these are financial and economic. Deloitte Access Economics, for example, has provided one calculation of the significant economic contribution that religious communities make to the country.[14] The relational or person-centred dimension which makes larger religious agencies attractive to government for formal service delivery also reflects a financial commitment, requiring resources to retain a stable body of staff and to support them in what is often relentlessly demanding work. Other under-appreciated aspects of the contribution that religious communities make to the building up of a decent society are not possible to quantify. Their significance is perhaps best grasped by imagining what their absence would mean for individuals and communities.

Religion is often mentioned as a factor in sustaining social cohesion. It is important to consider the different forms this takes. To begin with, there is a physical place—synagogue, temple, mosque, or church—where people can come together around shared belief and worship and the various activities to which they give rise. The importance of belonging to a place has re-emerged as a factor in politics, most dramatically perhaps in the arguments over the meaning the Brexit vote. We are rediscovering that having an actual place where you feel you belong is a crucial part of the sense of belonging and generates strong commitments, including commitments to action.

Feeling that you are part of something bigger than yourself makes activity worthwhile and meaningful. This is certainly the case for local religious communities, and when their activity is directed outwards it extends a sense of belonging to those who are not part of the worshipping community. This includes both those who are attracted to the outreach of these communities as volunteers, often without sharing the faith commitment of the community, and those they help, not least by easing feelings of isolation, abandonment, and powerlessness that attend prolonged loneliness, suffering, and hardship. This engagement with people who are struggling, whether it comes from a local religious community or from a larger religious service provider, can also play an important part in helping them to recover a measure of stability in their situation, and a sense that things can get better.

It is important to acknowledge, as Robert Hefner emphasises, that there can also be a "dark-side of religious (and other) solidarities in civil society": "it is not just the strength of association that matters, but the public ethical norms to which those in religious associations dedicate themselves". Where these norms and values "are exclusive or discriminatory, civil society networks and associations can become 'uncivil' and contribute not to the strengthening of an inclusive citizenship but to illiberal exclusions". The attachment or co-opting of religious traditions to different forms of populism or exclusivist nationalism in different places is perhaps the most prominent instance of this at the moment.

While agreeing with Turner about the way individualisation corrodes "the solidarities on which both democracies and religion depend", Hefner highlights the way other forces favour new forms of association and identification which exacerbate social polarisation and undermine civility, so compounding the problem. Some of these take religious forms or appropriate religious traditions. In Hefner's assessment, however, none of this "detracts from the fact that key features of religion in the modern West contributed to the inculcation of civil habits of the heart, as well as providing theological and ontological grounds for the affirmation for human dignity". It is because of their part in the practical continuation of this work that the examples given above are so important to recognise publicly and in policy, not least because of the way this important contribution can be obscured by the dark side of religious solidarities and the problems they pose.

Other issues are also at work in overshadowing this positive contribution of religion to democratic life. Jocelyne Cesari identifies a critical factor in the way we have conceptualised the distinction between the religious and the secular in political theory: the secular is understood as the cornerstone of collective life and politics, "while religion becomes personal spirituality". The history of religion's involvement in politics in the West continues to haunt the scene, leading to an insistence that religion should have no social or political influence (when of course it does), informed by a fear of religion reclaiming its ancient role in providing the "rules and meanings for the polis or community" (when its capacity to do any such thing in modern democracies is quite remote). Islam looms largest here in Western imaginations. Riaz Hassan observes that "Islamophobia emerges as a phobia of religion in the secular state", and in this Islam is made to stand for religion generally.

Cesari argues that political science approaches religions "almost exclusively as ideological phenomena, that is identified and studied primarily as ideas of beliefs" and as sources of political mobilisation, ". . . as if ideas and beliefs alone determine political situations". The gap that opens up as a consequence "between political reality and our theoretical tools" means that the important dimensions of "belonging and behaving" in religion are neglected, when "they are in some cases more significant" than belief. Focussing on belonging and behaving helps to correct the blind spot on religion for public policy in secular societies such as Australia, placing its negative impacts in a more complete context while also enabling clear-sightedness about the positive contributions religion makes to social life and to the mode, manner, and foundations of democratic life.

In its most significant aspect, this blind spot concerns how we sustain the values and forms of solidarity on which democratic life relies, if it is to realise some approximation of the common good. Democracy cannot generate them by itself (although it can provide an hospitable environment for them to grow if the seasons are good), and assumes that they will always be there because they always have been. Religion is not the only source of these values and forms of solidarity, and it can be an influence for evil as well as for good, like other forms of association and belief. Nevertheless, it remains one important source for them, and the gap that would be left if it were to disappear could not be easily filled. It would be expensive at the very least for government programs or corporations to try to substitute for what branches of the Society of St Vincent de Paul and similar organisations do in their own local areas, and doubtful that they could replicate the nature of the encounter between local people that occurs in its work.

Beyond this, however, are much larger and more worrying questions. From what sources does a secular society renew a commitment to universal equality of persons? How does it resist trends within itself to re-define personhood so that some categories of human beings are excluded from this protection? How does it sustain a commitment to those who are suffering or unjustly treated as a priority for a good society, against the powerful human tendency to venerate strength and dominate others? What compelling answer can it give—which is not residually Christian or religious—to the question, "Why should we care about the weak?"

To ask these questions is not to suggest that a secular society cannot answer them. There is still plenty of generosity, self-sacrifice, and care for others—mixed in with other things—in the various movements of our day. These are human attributes, after all, not exclusively religious attributes. The point is rather to highlight the complacency of secular societies about these sorts of questions and the values and sources of solidarity on which democratic life depends. Public policy needs to be more attentive to these matters, to what makes a decent society possible, to what strengthens and sustains it, and to what erodes it or slowly transforms it into something else. The positive contribution that religion and religious life makes to answering these questions warrants a broadening of public policy's focus to take them into account on their own terms, rather than taking them for granted.

Reflection is also required on the relationship between the positive contributions which are taken for granted, and the beliefs and practices of religious communities which are regarded with mistrust or treated as intolerable by secular societies. Is it possible to have one without the other? Secular societies assume that it is, and make this the basis for increasing supervision of religious communities and encroachments on the rights of individual believers.[15] As Turner notes, this is part of a larger development in secular societies, "in which the state exercises governance over what can count as 'a religion' and what is acceptable and unacceptable as 'religious behaviour'".

The other major problem identified in this volume is secular incomprehension towards religion. James Franklin describes succinctly one aspect of this problem: "Up to only yesterday, most people had a general idea of what religion was about and how religious people saw it bearing on ethics and public policy. Now they don't. A secular mindset has grown up that instantiates not just hostility to religion but an unteachable incomprehension of it". Franklin offers as an example of this "unteachable incomprehension" the way in which reasoned objections to certain medical procedures on moral or religious grounds made by some healthcare professionals are disparaged as dogma or superstition and dismissed as irrational.

Even if it is not always unteachable and hostile, a more or less generalised incomprehension of how religious convictions can inform people's approaches to ethics and public policy, and how this is not deeply suspect but entirely licit, is a common feature in many public discussions. Damien Freeman identifies five inter-related aspects to this larger incomprehension of religion in secular societies: religion's insistence that an adequate account of the world we live in must include a transcendent dimension; that ethics ultimately derive from metaphysics rather than from any particular human perspective; that "the nature of reality is such" that it imposes obligations which cannot be renounced; that "the individual in community" is "the most basic unit for thinking about what is fundamental to being human", not the individual alone and freed of relationships; and that human flourishing is not about the individual finding "personal meaning in a meaningless universe", but about the discovery of "the meaning inherent in the world" and ordering one's life in accordance with it.

As Freeman argues, expediency and necessity can overcome incomprehension to some extent, particularly in the area of politics. It is probably more accurate to say that this allows the problem to be managed and contained, rather than overcome, so that civic life is not completely ruptured. However, there needs to be a need—a practical imperative—for steps to be taken to manage and contain secular incomprehension, and even with this, "mutual suspicion, misunderstanding, and ambivalence" will remain.

Politics is pre-eminently the realm of the practical and the possible, not the perfect, and so forms of accommodation along these lines are not to be lamented if they secure peace and some measure of freedom and justice for both sides. Whether this is possible depends on a certain minimum of reasonableness, even if it only rises to the level of self-interest, which is not something that can be taken for granted in democratic societies. Earlier this century, governments in the United Kingdom and the United States preferred to have Catholic adoption and fostering agencies closed down (where they did not volunteer to secularise), against the interest that both government and society have in the invaluable work they did in a difficult, sensitive, and very important area, because they insisted on adhering to Catholic belief about marriage and family in their decisions.

Given the normalisation of this sort of extremism, it can be difficult to think of what sort of practical imperatives might induce secular societies to manage and limit their incomprehension of religion, particularly in the absence of the robust underlying commitment to live-and-let-live that still largely characterizes life in secular Australia, even if it has eroded significantly in some quarters. The surprising impact of religiously motivated voters on some issues is one example Freeman discusses, which is likely to become even more critical as the disposition against compromise with religion continues to harden among the elites. This is reinforced by Dean Smith's important observation about how the Australian system of compulsory voting and bicameralism helps to encourage moderation in politics—and in the public discussion of religion—and to ensure that a wide range of views, including religiously inspired views, are represented and heard in the Parliament.

An interesting possibility for overcoming secular and religious incomprehension lies in Michael Sandel's idea of the 'encumbered self'. As Freeman explains, there is incomprehension towards the encumbered self as well, arising primarily from the way in which we treat belief as a matter of choice rather than conviction. Liberalism protects religious freedom as a form of freedom of choice, but, in fact, religious freedom protects people in their beliefs about the truth and about what is right and wrong, and the obligations which these beliefs entail. The same is true for freedom of conscience.[16] Freeman describes how "we cannot change beliefs that we understand to be true, even if we desire to change them". Put more simply (in Sandel's words), "conscience dictates, choice decides". Conscience is a form of obligation, arising from convictions which encumber the self. Choice is an exercise of freedom. In the light of our belief in autonomy, it means that the individual alone is the source of any obligation, ensuring that the self remains unencumbered. As Freeman observes, such a view of choice and autonomy "will struggle to accommodate the perspective of other persons who believe themselves to be bound by duties that are not derived from themselves".

Rabbi David Saperstein raises a number of important questions about Sandel's idea and Freeman's use of it, seeing Sandel's formulation as substituting "claims of religious conscience" for "claims of religious choice." He raises four concerns about Sandel's argument: the role of choice in accepting the encumbrance of a belief and the obligations that follow from it; whether the idea of encumbrance works against the lived reality of human life in the freedom to change or abandon beliefs as our search for the truth continues; the fact that conscientious belief is not always and necessarily directed to the common good or the good of others, as these concepts would normally be understood in a democratic society; and the implications for civil rights if a priority is given to "claims of religious conscience" over rights-based claims. These important considerations further deepen the complexity involved in struggling to understand how some people come to a conclusion— which they see as something they are compelled to rather than an option they select—that leaves them with no choice in how they respond to a particular moral or religious question.

Freeman proposes that the struggle may be less difficult if the encumbered self is understood more broadly, to comprise not only those bound by obligations of conscience or moral or religious conviction, but also those whose attachments to place, attributes of identity, and special relationships of obligation decisively mark who they are, beyond any choosing. Indigenous Australians' attachment to country is not "a lifestyle choice", any more than the attachment and obligations of parents to their children. Sexuality and gender identification are also seen as attributes of identity which are not chosen.

Each of these examples represents a form of encumbered self. Treating them as choices, and therefore as matters that can be put to one side or overridden if other considerations demand it, is to require people to be false to themselves and to negate who they are.

Seen in this light, the encumbered self of conscience or religious conviction is not perhaps so incomprehensible to a secular society. Freeman argues that in different ways each of these examples reflects a form of encumbrance "beyond the control of one's will". It might be added that most of them also entail "duties derived from sources" other than the individual.

For all this, the encumbered self of religious conviction remains set apart. Each of the other examples Freeman gives can attract disparagement and hostility from different places and for different reasons, because of *who* the encumbered self is: an Indigenous Australian, a non-heterosexual, a transgender person, a parent. For those with religious or conscientious convictions, especially those at odds with the secular consensus and its enforceable understandings, the true object of resentment is not who they are— even if the shorthand might refer to a collective identity such as Catholic or Muslim—but *what* they believe. Their beliefs obviously shape who they are, and they may in part explain their adherence to their beliefs as a matter of being true to themselves. At bottom, however, they adhere to their beliefs because they feel compelled to adhere to the truth as something greater and more important than who they are.

A person who refuses to take innocent life or to participate in torture may well explain his reasons by saying he could not live with himself if he complied, and this would no doubt be true. But the reason he could not live with himself is precisely his conviction of the transcendent truth that torture and the taking of innocent life are always and everywhere wrong. The example is uncontroversial, but the key point here is not: for the transcendent is a source not only of incomprehension of religion for a secular society, but also of profound resentment for a world which reveres unencumbered autonomy—the individual as the sole source of his own duties or obligations—as the supreme value.

A more mundane aspect of the problem of incomprehension which Freeman identifies is comfort. Religious traditions arose in a world—the world of most of human history—"in which life is more readily characterised by woe, pain, misery, hunger, and despair". As modern societies have come to supplant this world with "a life of food, drink, and comfy sofas" for a very large majority of their populations, the need for the consolations of religion has ebbed away. The political scientist Ronald Inglehart makes the same point by placing the emphasis on security rather than comfort: "as societies develop, survival becomes more secure: starvation, once pervasive, becomes uncommon; life expectancy increases; murder and other forms of violence diminish. And as this level of security rises, people tend to become less religious".[17]

With the decline in the need for consolation, people become less dependent on religion "and less willing to accept its constraints", particularly in the area of sexuality and fertility as life expectancy increases and infant mortality declines. The "pro-fertility norms" of religions which were necessary when life expectancy was low and infant mortality high gradually become redundant—and then incomprehensible—as new generations grow up taking their security for granted.[18] As the old religious constraints fall away, surveys show they are replaced in secular countries by "an equally strong set of norms" prioritising "self-expression and free choice", with a growing emphasis on human rights, the environment, and gender equality. In contrast to contemporary political tribalism and cancel culture, tolerance of "outsiders" and "freedom of speech" are also meant to be valued by the rising secular generation.[19]

If the rise of comfort and security has helped to make religion incomprehensible to people in secular societies, the decline of faith in these circumstances remains in many ways incomprehensible to religious people. While the world in developed countries has become much more hospitable physically, "woe, pain, misery, [existential] hunger, and despair" have not departed the human condition. They have taken on some new forms while continuing many of the old, causing anguish and dread no less terrible for people who are otherwise physically secure and comfortable. The need for consolation remains, but it is a consolation that religion seems no longer able to provide as powerfully or as broadly as it once did. This incomprehension that religious people feel is only deepened by the way that more humane conditions seem to have reduced not only the power of religion's consolations but the appeal of its promises of happiness or fulfilment in this life as well. Despite the contribution that the triumph of autonomy has made (for example) to loneliness becoming a distinctive feature of the secular world, or to various forms of bitterness and regret between men and women, what Christianity sees and offers as a better way for community and relationships has only limited attraction.

Overcoming the blind spots and incomprehension that secular society has towards religion can be helped or hindered by how we approach them. Luke Gosling argues that it is an advantage if "we have leaders who help others to see the constructive intuitions" in the religious traditions in our society, and the contribution they make to civility, the rebuilding of trust, and a deeper vision of the common good. Receptiveness and generosity are also important, and a willingness to overcome divides and differences, rather than a determination to deepen them. We know how easy it is to deepen divides at the moment. Working from superseded presuppositions that religion is over, that it has nothing to offer a modern democracy except prejudice and extremism, and that secular society can only be a higher form of civilisation, self-sufficient and self-renewing, does not help to overcome divides. Looking upon the secular dispensation as a form of loss or falling way, as something that, through its drift away from religion and the transcendent, inevitably diminishes or trivialises what it means to be human, is not helpful either. Our lot, as Casanova argues, is to live in a world that is becoming at once more religious and more secular. We need to come to grips with this reality and take some new bearings. How open we are to doing so will determine the possibilities for rethinking the relationship between religion and secular society, which now stands as an essential task for the future of democracy in a religious world.

Contributors

Michael Casey is the director of the PM Glynn Institute, Australian Catholic University's public policy think-tank.

Jocelyne Cesari is the T. J. Dermot Dunphy visiting professor of religion, violence, and peacebuilding in the Harvard Divinity School and professor of religion and politics and director of research at the Edward Cadbury Centre for the Public Understanding of Religion in the University of Birmingham.

James Franklin is an honorary professor in the School of Mathematics and Statistics at the University of New South Wales.

Damien Freeman is principal policy advisor and general editor of the Kapunda Press at the PM Glynn Institute.

Luke Gosling OAM is the member for Solomon in the Parliament of the Commonwealth of Australia.

Riaz Hassan AM is an Australian Research Council professorial fellow and emeritus professor of sociology at Flinders University and senior honorary fellow at the Asia Institute, University of Melbourne.

Robert Hefner is a professor of anthropology and international relations in the Pardee School of Global Affairs at Boston University.

Rabbi the Honourable **David Saperstein** is president of the World Union for Progressive Judaism, director emeritus of the Religious Action Centre of Reform Judaism, adjunct professor at the Georgetown University School of Foreign Service's Centre for Jewish Civilization, a distinguished fellow of the PM Glynn Institute, and previously served as the United States Ambassador-at-Large for International Religious Freedom (2015-2017).

Dean Smith is a Senator for Western Australia in the Parliament of the Commonwealth of Australia and Chief Government Whip in the Senate.

The Honourable **Ursula Stephens** is the CEO of Catholic Social Services Australia.

Bryan Turner is a professor of sociology and a distinguished fellow of the PM Glynn Institute at Australian Catholic University, emeritus professor at the Graduate Center, City University of New York, and a member of the Academy of Social Sciences in Australia.

Notes

Introduction: Waves of democracy and religion in global history

1   S.P. Huntington, "Democracy's Third Wave", *Journal of Democracy*, 1991, Vol. 2(2), pp. 12-34.

2   *Ibid.*, p. 13.

3   *Ibid.*, p. 15.

Liberal societies in a religious world

1   J. Casanova, *Public Religions in the Modern World* (University of Chicago Press, 1994).

2   R. Bellah, "Civil Religion in America", *Journal of the American Academy of Arts and Sciences,* Vol. 96(1), pp. 1-21.

3   G. Fitzi, J. Mackert, Juergen and B.S. Turner (eds), *Populism and the Crisis of Democracy* (Routledge, 2019), 3 volumes.

4   D. Lehmann, *Struggle for the Spirit: Religious Transformation and Popular Culture in Brazil and Latin America* (Polity Press, 1996).

5   R. Forlenza, "The Enemy Within: Catholic Anti-Communism in Cold War Italy", *Past & Present,* 2017, Vol. 235, pp. 207-42; R. Forlenza, "New Perspectives on Twentieth Century Catholicism", *Contemporary European History,* 2019, Vol. 28(4), pp. 581-95.

6   S. Moyn, *The Last Utopia: Human Rights in History* (Belknap Press, 2010).

7   A. de Tocqueville, *Democracy in America and Two Essays on America,* transl. G.E. Bevan (Penguin, 2003 [1835 and 1840]).

8   J. Cesari, *Why the West Fears Islam: An Exploration of Muslims in Liberal Democracies* (Palgrave Macmillan, 2013).

9   N. Glazer, *We are all multiculturalists now* (Harvard University Press, 1997).

10 F. Gauthier, Religion, *Modernity, Globalisation: Nation-State to Market* (Routledge, 2020).

11 B.S. Turner, *Religion and Modern Society: Citizenship, Secularisation and the State* (Cambridge University Press, 2011), p. 279.

12 R. Stark and W. Bainbridge, *A Theory of Religion* (Peter Lang, 1987).

13 D. Horne, *The Lucky Country* (Penguin, 1964).

14 F. Mansouri, M. Lobo, and A. Johns, "Grounding Religiosity in Urban Space: insights from multicultural Melbourne", *Australian Geographer,* 2016, Vol.

47(3), pp. 295-310.

15 S. Dagistanli, A. Possamai, B.S. Turner, M. Voyce, and J. Roose, "The limits of multiculturalism in Australia? The Shari'a flogging case of R v Raad, Fayed, Cifci and Coskun", *Sociological Review,* 2018, pp 1-18.

16 S. Newfield, *Degrees of Separation: Identity Formation in Ultra-Orthodox Judaism* (Temple University Press, 2020).

17 R. Hassan, *Islamophobia, social distance and fear of terrorism in Australia* (International Centre for Muslim and non-Muslim Understanding, 2015); R. Hassan, *Australian Muslims: the challenge of Islamophobia and social distance* (International Centre for Muslim and non-Muslim Understanding, 2018).

18 *Australian Muslims*, p. 13.

19 R. Camus, *La Grand Remplacement* (D. Reinarc, 2011).

20 E. Kaufmann, *Whiteshift: Populism, Immigration and the Future of White Majorities* (Allen Lane, 2018).

21 S. Brake and L.M.H. Aguilar, "'They love death as we love life': The 'Muslim Question' and the biopolitics of replacement", *British Journal of Sociology,* 2020, pp. 1-22.

22 R. Lesthaeghe, "The Unfolding Story of the Second Demographic Transition", *Population and Development Review,* 2010, Vol. 36(2), pp. 211-251.

23 W. Kymlicka, "Review: Theorizing Indigenous Rights (Indigenous Peoples in International Law by S. James Anaya)", *University of Toronto Law Journal,* 1999, Vol. 49(2), pp. 281-293.

24 W. Kymlicka, *Multicultural Citizenship: A Liberal Theory of Minority Rights* (Oxford University Press, 1995).

25 Hudson and Keane (eds), *Rethinking Australian Citizenship* (Cambridge University Press, 2000).

26 B. Wilson, *Religion in Secular Society,* ed. S Bruce, new edn (Oxford University Press, 2016 [1966]).

27 J. Casanova, *Public Religions in the Modern World* (University of Chicago Press, 1994).

28 P.L. Berger, *The Sacred Canopy: Resurgent Religion and World Politics* (Anchor Books, 1967).

29 P.L. Berger, *The Desecularization of the World: Resurgent Religion and World Politics* (William B. Eerdmans Publishing Company, 1999).

30 D. Lehmann, *Struggle for the Spirit: Religious Transformation and Popular Culture in Brazil and Latin America* (Polity Press, 1996).

31 D. Martin, *Pentecostalism: The World Their Parish* (Blackwell, 2002).

32 A. Possamai-Iniseldy, *Alphia and Nixon, Digital Social;Religion and Belief* (De Gruyter, 2019).

33 A. Possamai (ed.), *Handbook of Hyper-Real Religion* (Brill, 2012).

34 K. Dempsey, *To Comfort and Challenge: the role of the Church in an Australian Country* (La Trobe Sociology Papers, 1977); K. Dempsey, *Conflict and Decline: ministers and laymen in an Australian Town* (Methuen, 1983).

35 E. Fry (ed.), *Rebels and Radicals* (George Allen & Unwin, 1983).

36 E. Shils, "Ideology and civility: On the Politics of the Intellectual", *Sewanee Review*, 1958, Vol. 66(3), pp. 450-480.

37 J. Arditi, *A Genealogy of Manners* (Chicago University Press, 1998); N. Elias, *The Civilizing Process* (Wiley, 2000).

38 O. Jones, *Chavs: The Demonization of the Working Class* (Verso, 2016).

39 J.Q., Whitman, "Civility and respect: three societies", *Yale Law Journal*, 2000, Vol. 109(6), pp. 1279-1398.

40 C. Lapavitsas, "The Financialization of Capitalism: profiting without producing", *City*, 2013, Vol. 17(6), pp. 792-805.

41 A. Case and A. Deaton, *Mortality and Morbidity in the 21st Century* (Brookings Papers on Economic Activity, 2017)

42 D. Ging, "Alphas, Betas, and Incels: theorizing the masculinities of the Manosphere", *Men and Masculinities*, 2017, Vol. 22(4), pp.638-657.

43 B.S. Turner, "Trump, religion and populism" in G. Fitzi, J. Mackert and B.S. Turner (eds), *Populism and the Crisis of Democracy* (Routledge, 2019), Vol. 3, pp. 168-179.

44 R.P. Jones, *The End of White Christian America* (Simon & Schuster, 2016).

45 E. Monk-Turner, "White Evangelical Activists and the Gender Divide in the 2016 Presidential Election", *Society*, 2020, Vol. 57, pp. 30-40.

46 R. Forlenza and B. S. Turner, "Das Abendland: The Politics of Europe's Religious Borders", *Critical Research on Religion*, 2019, Vol. 7(1), pp. 6-23.

47 R. Scruton, *Our Church: A Personal History of the Church of England* (Atlantic Books, 2013).

48 G.D. Bouma, "Islamophobia as a constraint to world peace: the case of Australia", *Islam and Christian-Muslim Relations*, 2011, Vol. 22(4), pp. 433-441.

49 M. Maddox, *God Under Howard: the rise of the religious right in Australian Politics* (Allen & Unwin, 2005).

50 A. Summers, *Damned Whores and God's Police* (NewSouth Books, 2016 [1975]).

51 R.W. Connell and J.W. Messerschmidt, "Hegemonic Masculinity—rethinking the concept", *Gender and Society*, 2005, Vol. 19(6), pp. 829-859.

52 J. Barbalet, and B.S. Turner (eds), *Religion and the State: A comparative sociology* (Anthem, 2011).

53 A. Possamai-Inesedy and B.S. Turner, "Same-Sex Marriage and the Christian Conservative Reaction" in J.-G.A. Goulet (ed.), *Religious Diversity Today: Experiencing Religion in the Contemporary World* (Praeger, 2016), Vol. 3, pp. 203-228.

54 B.S. Turner and Y. Contreras-Vejar, "Happiness" in B.S. Turner (ed.), *Wiley Blackwell Encyclopedia of Social Theory* (Wiley Blackwell, 2018), Vol. III, pp. 1030-1037.

55 D. Bok, *The Politics of Happiness* (Princeton University Books, 2010), p. 23.

56 R. Veenhoven, *Conditions of Happiness* (Springer, 1984).

57 J. Helliwell, R. Layard and J. Sachs (eds), *World Happiness Report* (United Nations: OECD, 2015).

58 R.L. Miles, *Happiness, Holiness and the Moral Life in John Wesley* (Cambridge University Books, 2009), Part III: Wesley's Work.

59 1 Corinthians 15:14.

Democratic leaders in a religious world

1 M. Gluckman, *Custom and Conflict in Africa* (Blackwell, 1973), p. 76; I am indebted to Dr Ronald Hyam, a fellow of Magdalene College, Cambridge, for drawing this and the following quotation from C. S. Lewis to my attention: *vide* R. Hyam, *Empire and Sexuality: The British experience* (Manchester University Press, 1990), p. 183.

2 C.S. Lewis, *The Allegory of Love: A study in Medieval tradition* (Oxford University Press, 1936), p. 4.

3 *Ibid.*, p. 3.

4 J. Norman, "The moral basis of a commercial society" in D. Freeman (ed.), *The Market's Morals: Responding to Jesse Norman* (Kapunda Press, 2019), pp. 1-18, pp. 13-14.

5 E. Burke, "Thoughts on the Cause of the Present Discontents" (1770) in *Reflections on the Revolution in France and other writings*, ed. J. Norman (Everyman, 2015), p. 113.

6 Pew Research Center, "The Future of World Religions: Population Growth Projections, 2010-2050", 2 April 2015.

7 J. D. Heydon, "Religious 'toleration' in modern Australia: the tyranny of tolerance" in D. Freeman (ed.), *Today's Tyrants: Responding to Dyson Heydon* (Kapunda, 2018), pp. 3-20.

8 F. Brennan, "A history of respectful debate" in D. Freeman (ed.), *Today's Tyrants: Responding to Dyson Heydon* (Kapunda, 2018), pp. 21-34.

9 "On the whole, people of faith did not desert Labor, but Labor lost some support among Christian voters – particularly devout, first-generation migrant Christians.": C. Emerson and J. Wetherall (chairs), Review of Labor's 2019 Federal Election Campaign, p. 8. See also A. Patty, "Christian leaders say religious freedom was among issues that influenced voters", *Sydney Morning Herald*, 20 May 2019, and A. West, "How religious voters lost faith in Labor: Lessons from the 2019 federal

election", ABC Religion & Ethics, 24 May 2019: <www.abc.net.au/religion/how-religious-voters-lost-faith-in-labor/11146850>.

10 J. Brotton, *The Sultan and the Queen: the untold story of Elizabeth and Islam* (Viking, 2016), p. 8.

11 *Ibid.*, pp. 10-11.

12 *Ibid.*, p. 299.

13 R. Curtis, B. Elton, R. Atkinson, and J. Lloyd, *Blackadder: The Whole Damn Dynasty, 1485-1917* (Penguin, 1999), p. 328.

14 M.J. Sandel, "Religious Liberty—Freedom of Conscience or Freedom of Choice", *Utah Law Review*, 1989, pp. 597-616.

15 Cf. G. Craven, "Protecting religious freedom" in F. Brennan, M.A. Casey, and G. Craven, *Chalice of Liberty: protecting religious freedom in Australia* (Kapunda Press, 2018), pp. 57-95.

16 Sandel, p. 611.

17 *Thornton v Caldor, Inc* 472 US 703 (1985) is given as an example of a decision that treats religious freedom as a matter of protecting unencumbered selves, whereas *Wisconsin v Yoder* 406 US 205 (1972) is given as an example of a decision that treats religious freedom as a matter of protecting encumbered selves.

18 S. Medhora, "Remote communities are 'lifestyle choices', says Tony Abbott", *Guardian Australia*, 10 March 2015.

19 J. Sacks, *The Dignity of Difference: How to avoid the clash of civilizations*, revised edn (Continuum, 2003), p. 11.

20 *Ibid.*, p. 15.

21 *Ibid.*, p. 151.

22 *Ibid.*, p. 20.

23 *Ibid.*, p. 21.

24 R. Williams, "Overcoming political tribalism" in D. Freeman, *Tribalism's Troubles: Responding to Rowan Williams* (Kapunda Press, 2020).

25 Sacks, p. 47.

26 *Ibid.*, p. 50.

27 *Ibid.*, p. 52.

28 *Ibid.*, p. 61.

29 *Ibid.*, p. 62.

30 I. Berlin, *Liberty* (Oxford, 2002), p. 345; as cited in Sacks, p. 63.

31 Sacks, p. 82.

32 F. Fukuyama, *The End of History and the Last Man* (Hamish Hamilton, 1992), p. 332; as cited in Sacks, pp. 198-99.

33 Sacks, pp. 201-02.

34 *Ibid.*, p. 204.

35 *Ibid.*, p. 199.

36 *Ibid.*, p. 200.

37 *Ibid.*, p. 41.

38 *Ibid.*, pp. 193-94.

39 *Ibid.*, p. 195.

Responding to Bryan Turner and Damien Freeman

1. Amen to Holy Land in Australia

1 See C.S. Lewis, *The Abolition of Man; or, Reflections on Education with Special Reference to the Teaching of English in the Upper Forms of Schools* (1942).

2 A. Creighton, "Left's view shows it's time for another Labor split", *The Australian,* 20 June 2020.

2. Accommodating religion in Australian democracy

1 Section 116 of the Australian Constitution.

2 G. Melluish, "Religion and politics in Australia", *Political Theology,* 2010, Vol. 11(6).

3 C. Puplik, "The case for compulsory voting", *The People's say: Elections in Australia* (Australian Electoral Commission, 1994).

4 Evans and Laing, *Odgers Australian Senate Practice,* 12th edn (2012), p. 1.

5 *The Federalist,* No. 62 (Everyman, 1970), pp. 317-318.

6 Evans and Laing, p. 3.

3. Leadership and society in a less monochromatic world

1 C. McCrudden, *Litigating Religions: An Essay on Human Rights, Courts and Beliefs* (Oxford University Press, 2018), pp. 6-7.

2 E. Erenchinova and E. Proudchenko, "Spirituality and Moral Values", SHS Web of Conferences, 2018, Vol. 50: see <https://www.shs-conferences.org/articles/shsconf/pdf/2018/11/shsconf_cildiah2018_01050.pdf>.

3 G. Miller, "Social distancing prevents infections, but it can have unintended consequences", *Science,* 16 March 2020: see <https://www.sciencemag.org/news/2020/03/we-are-social-species-how-will-social-distancing-affect-us>.

4 H. Kushner, *Who Needs God?* (Summit Books, 1989), p. 209.

4. Faith's place in an age of democratic trial

1   I am adopting this phrase and its connotations from Charles Taylor, *A Secular Age* (Harvard University Press, 2007).

2   My phrasing is intended to evoke Arthur Kleinman's vivid analysis of the challenge of ethical prioritisation in contemporary China. See A.A. Kleinman, *What Really Matters: Living a Moral Life Amidst Uncertainty and Danger* (Oxford University Press, 2007).

3   A. Stepan, "The Multiple Secularisms of Modern Democratic and non-Democratic Regimes" in C. Calhoun, M. Juergensmeyer and J. Van Antwerpen (eds), *Rethinking Secularism* (Oxford University Press, 2011), pp. 114-144, p. 116.

4   *Ibid.*, p. 114.

5   The phrase "assertive secularist" is from Ahmet Kuru's study of secularism in France, the United States, and Turkey, and refers to varieties of secularist governance that enforce strong prohibitions against the presence of religious institutions in public life. See A.T. Kuru, *Secularism and State Policies Toward Religion: The United States, France, and Turkey* (Cambridge University Press, 2009).

6   Stepan, pp. 114-115.

7   *Ibid.*, p. 117.

8   J. Fox, "World Separation of Religion and State into the 21st Century", *Comparative Political Studies*, 2006, Vol. 39, pp. 537-569, p. 537.

9   Stepan, p. 117.

10   J. Fox, "Separation of Religion and State in Stable Christian Democracies: Fact or Myth?", *Journal of Law, Religion and State*, 2012, Vol. 1, pp. 60-94.

11   *Ibid.*, p. 86.

12   Kuru, p. 78.

13   *Ibid.*, p. 85.

14   *Ibid.*, p. 86.

15   R. McVeigh, *The Rise of the Ku Klux Klan: Right-wing Movements and National Politics* (University of Minnesota Press, 2009).

16   J. Beaman, "Citizenship as Cultural: Towards a Theory of Cultural Citizenship", *Sociology Compass*, 2016, Vol. 10, pp. 849-857.

17   T.B. Hansen, *The Saffron Wave: Democracy and Hindu Nationalism in Modern India* (Princeton University Press, 1999).

18   See R.W. Hefner, *Democratic Civility: The History and Cross-Cultural Possibility of a Modern Political Ideal* (Rutgers University Press, 1998).

19   T.B. Hansen "Democracy against the Law: Reflections on India's Illiberal Democracy" in A.P. Chatterji, T.B. Hansen, and C. Jaffrelots (eds), *Majoritarian State: How Hindu Nationalism is Changing India* (Oxford University Press, 2019), pp. 19-39, p. 21.

20 See G. Fitzi, J. Mackert and B.S. Turner, *Populism and the Crisis of Democracy* (Routledge, 2019), Vol. 1: Concepts and Theory.

21 See A. MacIntyre, *After Virtue: A Study in Moral Theory*, 3rd edn (University of Notre Dame Press, 2007).

22 J.A. Laidlaw, *The Subject of Virtue: An Anthropology of Ethics and Freedom* (Cambridge University Press, 2014), p. 62.

23 See S. Schielke, *Egypt in Future Tense: Hope, Frustration, and Abivalence Before and after 2011* (Indiana University Press, 2015).

24 C. Hallisey, "Ethical Particularism in Theravada Buddhism", *Journal of Buddhist Ethics*, 1996, Vol. 3, pp. 32-43; and S. Ahmed, *What is Islam? The Importance of Being Islamic* (Princeton University Press, 2016).

25 See R.W. Hefner (ed), *Shari'a Law and Modern Muslim Ethics* (Indiana University Press, 2016).

26 C. Taylor, "How to Define Secularism" in A. Stepan and C. Taylor (eds), *Boundaries of Toleration* (Columbia University Press, 2014), pp. 59-78, p. 61.

27 *Ibid.*, p. 68.

28 *Ibid.*, p. 70.

29 *Ibid.*, p. 63.

30 *Ibid.*, p. 68.

5. Democracy in a religious world or religion in a democratic world?

1 J. Cesari, *What Is Political Islam?* (Lynne Rienner Publishers, 2018); J. Cesari and J. Casanova, *Islam, Gender and Democracy in Comparative Perspective* (Oxford University Press, 2017); J. Cesari, *We God's People: Christianity, Islam and Hinduism in a World of Nations* (Cambridge University Press, forthcoming).

2 E. Durkheim, *The Elementary Forms of the Religious Life* (Simon & Schuster Ltd, 1995).

3 *Ibid.*

4 For an analysis of this shift of the sacred toward the national community, see J. Cesari, "Time, Power and Religion: Comparing the Temple Mount and the Ayodhya Disputes", *Journal of Law, Religion and Society,* forthcoming.

5 E. Mendieta and J. Beaumont, "Reflexive Secularization" in J. Beaumont (ed.), *The Routledge Handbook of Postsecularity* (Routledge, 2018), pp. 425-436.

6 *Ibid.*

7 C. Taylor, *A Secular Age,* (Harvard University Press, 2007).

8 J. Cesari, *What Is Political Islam?;* J. Cesari, "Unexpected Convergences: Religious Nationalism in Israel and Turkey", *Religions,* 2018, Vol. 9(11), p. 334.

9 C. Taylor, *A Secular Age.*

10 *Ibid.*

11 H. Ināyat, *Modern Islamic Political Thought* (University of Texas Press, 1982);

I.M. Lapidus, *A History of Islamic Societies* (Cambridge University Press, 1988).

12 A.H. Hourani, *Arabic Thought in the Liberal Age: 1798-1939* (Oxford University Press, 1962).

13 T. Madood, *Multicultural Politics: Racism, Ethnicity, and Muslims in Britain* (University of Minnesota Press, 2005).

14 "Shari'a Law 'Could Have UK Role'", BBC News, 4 July 2008, see: <http://news.bbc.co.uk/2/hi/uk_news/7488790.stm>.

15 J. Cesari, *Why the West Fears Islam: An Exploration of Muslims in Liberal Democracies* (Palgrave Macmillan, 2013).

16 R. Brubaker. "Between Nationalism and Civilizationism: The European Populist Movement in Europe in Comparative Perspective", *Ethnic and Racial Studies,* 2017, Vol. 40(8), p. 1204.

6. Religious freedom in the twenty-first century

1 United States Constitution, Amendment 1.

2 See M.J. Sandel, "Religious Liberty—Freedom of Conscience or Freedom of Choice," *Utah Law Review,* 1989, pp. 599-605.

3 "Jefferson's Letter to the Danbury Baptists" (1802): <https://www.loc.gov/loc/lcib/9806/danpre.html>.

4 United Nations General Assembly. *Universal Declaration of Human Rights* (1948) and United Nations General Assembly, *International Covenant on Civil and Political Rights* (1966).

5 J. Sacks, *The Dignity of Difference: How to Avoid the Clash of Civilizations* (Continuum, 2002).

6 One thread running through Turner's discussion of multiculturalism is recognition of parallel law systems. In the United States, in passing legislation, religious law only plays a role when it is coextensive with secular justifications accessible to all, justifications not only accessible as a matter of faith but through rational discourse. If that is true, the fact religious doctrines coincide with secular justification does not delegitimize the law. But religious law per se cannot be the sole basis of United States law and the Supreme Court has struck down laws based entirely on religious belief as violations of the Establishment Clause.

What we do have is a number of 'alternative dispute resolution' mechanisms that use other sources of law to adjudicate primarily non-criminal disputes. These function as a voluntary binding arbitration process. So if two ultra-orthodox Jews have a business dispute, rather than sue each other in civil court, they can voluntarily decide to do so in a *bet din* (a Jewish law court) to resolve the dispute under Jewish law; so too a Muslim could go to a Shari'a court. If the two parties before the court agree voluntarily to abide by the decision of the religious court, then a civil court will enforce that judgment, just as it would a secular arbitration panel—but will not get involved in judging or interpreting the religious law merits of that holding. This allows people to live in accordance with their religious beliefs in resolving any kind of dispute that might otherwise bring them into civil court. Interesting to note is that Jewish law itself has a related kind of provision. With Jews living in so many different countries under so many different governing authorities, the rabbinic rule devised 2,000 years ago in the early period of the Talmud is *dina d'malchuta dina*—the law of the land is the law that Jews follow unless it requires violating Jewish ritual law or the controlling legal system is inherently discriminatory against Jews.

7   Pew Forum, "Muslims in America: Immigrants and those born in U.S. see life differently in many ways", 17 April 2018.

8   See W. Herberg, *Catholic, Protestant, Jew,* (University of Chicago Press, 1955, 1960, 1983); D.P. Moynihan and N. Glazer, *Beyond the Melting Pot* (MIT Press, 1970). For Zangwill's play that popularised the concept of 'the melting pot', see I. Zangwill, *The Melting Pot* (Macmillan, 1909).

9   R. Bellah, W.M Sullivan, R. Madsen, A. Swidler and S.M.Tipton, *Habits of the Heart* (University of California, 1985).

10 Anti-Defamation League, "Antisemitic Attitudes in the U.S.: A Guide to ADL's Latest Poll": <https://www.adl.org/survey-of-american-attitudes-toward-jews#introduction>.

11 Southern Poverty Law Center, "Hate Map": <https://www.splcenter.org/hate-map>.

12 Federal Bureau of Investigation, 2018 Hate Crime Statistics: <https://ucr.fbi.gov/hate-crime/2018>.

13 *2019 American Values Atlas* (Public Religion Research Institute).

14 *Lyng v Northwest Indian Cemetery Protective Association* 485 U.S. 439, (1988).

15 Exec. Order No. 13007, 3 C.F.R. p. 26771-26772 (1996).

16 Thinking more generally about the policies of President Trump, I have several concerns about Professor Turner's analysis of Trump's populism. Let me start with his argument about Jews—that President Trump's right-wing populism receives support from increased numbers of Jews given his "plan for Palestine and his attitude towards Israel." By the time this is printed, the 2020 election will be history and we will have more formal statistics. But throughout President Trump's presidency, Jews remained overwhelmingly anti-Trump—indeed, one of the most anti-Trump groups according to the polls. It is true that Orthodox Jews are more inclined to support him because of his support for Israel and because they get funding for their religious institutions from his administration (which is pushing the long standing limits on governmental funding for religious institutions that the courts had long held were required by the Establishment Clause). But even the Orthodox Jewish community does not like his personal behaviour and is not like the Christian religious right on a number of divisive issues in American politics: abortion, public school prayer, teaching 'creationism,' civil rights, or economic justice issues.

Professor Turner argues that early forms of populism emerged in the United States in the 1860s but contemporary interest in populism dates from the financial crisis of 2008-2011. I see the forces driving contemporary populism in far more long-term time wise and far broader in the number of causes that formulation suggests. The dynamics from which American populism flows are matched by trends in numerous democratic (and even non-democratic) nations. Let me mention a few in the American context:

a. Economic unease did not begin with the 2008 crisis. I see the confluence of three factors driving populism going back to the 1970s. Where in the post-WWII 1940s-60s, there was an explosive growth in the middle class, significant improvement of the economic state of minority groups, and a closing of the gap between the rich and the poor, since the 1970s, the pace of economic growth of the middle class, of wages generally, and the closing of the income gap have all declined or reversed.

b. Add to the economic factors, the related fears from those who warned of immigrants flooding in and taking over jobs stoking the right's "replacement" arguments. After 9/11, xenophobia had struck many segments of American society.

c. The growth beginning in the 1970s of the confluence of the religious right who cloaked a very conservative political agenda in religious garb, rhetoric, and culture, redefining what an authentic (particularly) Christian was like.

d. And finally, the fear and helplessness of some who recognise the end of white Christian America is already at hand and the end of a white majority America within their children's lifetime, if not their own. President Trump's 'Make America Great Again' slogan struck a deep chord of wanting to return things to the way they had been—an impossibility, but he clearly identified with (or at least used) their pain and their fears.

17 See <https://www.newsy.com/stories/a-broken-trust-sexual-assault-and-justice-on-tribal-lands/>.

18 See <https://digitalcommons.law.byu.edu/cgi/viewcontent. cgi?article=3202&context=lawreview>; and https://www.newsobserver.com/ news/politics-government/election/article246311535.html>.

19 "Because religious liberty protections have so often failed in the courts to deliver meaningful protections to distinctive Native American religious traditions, Native communities and their advocates have looked beyond the First Amendment and religious freedom law to accommodations under either federal Indian law, or under federal Indian law in concert with other legal regimes, such as historic preservation, environmental law, or Native specific statutes like the Native American Grave Protection and Repatriation Act (NAGPRA)." Congress has also failed to adequately fund tribes." See "Broken Promises", United States

Commission on Civil Rights: <https://www.usccr.gov/pubs/2018/12-20-Broken-Promises.pdf>.

20 Several European countries or individual states within EU countries have banned or limited kosher slaughter or are considering doing so:: see the Law Library of Congress, Global Legal Research Center, "Legal Restrictions on Religious Slaughter in Europe" (March 2018, updated September 2019). It is worth noting that in September 2020, the advocate general of the Court of Justice of the European Union advised the Court to prohibit European governments from banning kosher and halal slaughter: see C. Lipshiz, "EU court consultant: Countries should not be allowed to ban kosher, halal meat", Jewish Telegraphic Agency, 10 September 2020. On the issue of circumcision, some Icelandic legislators proposed a ban in 2018 but the effort was abandoned because of strong opposition both internationally and from key government leaders domestically. Denmark is set to debate a bill outlawing circumcision during its 2020-2021 parliamentary session: see C. Lipshiz, "Danish parliament to debate bill that would ban non-medical circumcision", *The Forward*, 8 September 2020.

21 M.R. Konvitz, *Judaism and the American Idea* (Cornell University Press, 1978), p. 38.

22 See J. Rabinowitz, *Jewish Law: Its Influence on the Development of Legal Institutions* (L.Bloch Publishing, 1956).

23 For the economic explanation for the return of the Jews to England, see C. Roth, *A History of the Jews in England*, 2nd edn (Schoken Books, 1961), p. 301. For the ideological explanation, see P. Johnson, *A History of the Jews* (Harper & Row, 1987), pp. 276-277.

24 R.D. Putnam, *Bowling Alone: The Collapse and Revival of American Community* (Simon & Schuster, 2000).

25 R.D. Putnam and D. Campbell, *American Grace: How Religion Divides and Unites Us* (Simon & Schuster, 2012).

26 *Ibid.*, also Pew Research Center, "America's Changing Religious Landscape", Pew Forum, 12 May 2015. The Pew Report states:

As the shifting religious profiles of these generational cohorts suggest, switching religion is a common occurrence in the United States. If all Protestants were treated as a single religious group, then fully 34% of American adults currently have a religious identity different from the one in which they were raised. This is up six points since 2007, when 28% of adults identified with a religion different from their childhood faith. If switching among the three Protestant traditions (e.g., from mainline Protestantism to the evangelical tradition, or from evangelicalism to a historically black Protestant denomination) is added to the total, then the share of Americans who currently have a different religion than they did in childhood rises to 42%.

27 *Ibid.*

28 Sandel, *op. cit.*

29 As to resisting oppressive states, certainly one can think of examples where the encumbered selves connected with sources of the good that were indispensable in resisting and defeating tyranny. But we can think equally of where those unencumbered selves, protected by and imbued with the structure of internationally recognised human rights, were able to free themselves of the groupthink of oppression, where their sense of their rights from within themselves empowered them to stand against evil. And, paradoxically, are not those in the latter category both unencumbered in Sandel's terms, even as their commitment to the regime of international human rights, to the legal, political, and social structures that inform those rights, to the religious streams who resonate with those rights another form of encumbrance?

30 See D. Saperstein, "Masterpiece Cakeshop: Impact on the Search for Common Ground" in W.N. Eskridge Jr and R.F. Wilson (eds), *Religious Freedom, LGBT Rights, and the Prospects for Common Ground* (Cambridge University Press, 2019), pp. 479-498.

31 Sacks is alluding to the biblical covenant with Noah standing in agency for all humankind through which the rabbis derive a set of universal ethical norms for people and societies—among them against killing, stealing, and sexual crimes, and the requirement of every nation and community to create courts of justice (which one can understand as calling for the creation of a system embodying the rule of law).

7. Islamophobia and secularism in liberal democracies

1 M. Mann, *The Dark Side of Democracy* (Cambridge University Press, 2005).

2 *Ibid.*

3 S.H. Alatas, *The Myth of the Lazy Native* (Routledge, 2014); Mann, *The Dark Side of Democracy.*

4 J. Casanova, *Public Religions in the Modern World* (University of Chicago Press, 1994).

5 *Ibid*; see also T. Asad, *Formations of the Secular: Christianity, Islam and Modernity* (Stanford University Press, 2003).

6 N. Luhmann, *The Differentiation of Society* (Columbia University Press, 1982).

7 R. Hassan, *Inside Muslim Minds* (Melbourne University Press, 2008), Chapter 4.

8 E. Gellner, *Conditions of Liberty* (Penguin Books, 1994).

9 K. Zebiri, "Orientalist themes in British Islamophobia" in J.L. Esposito an I. Kalin (eds) *Islamophobia: The Challenge of Pluralism in the 21st Century* (Oxford University Press, 2011).

10 G. Bouma, "Islamophobia as a Constraint to World Peace: the Case of Australia", *Islam and Christian-Muslim Relations,* 2011, Vol. 22(4), pp. 433–441.

11 J. Cesari, "Islamophobia in the West; A Comparsion between Europe and the

United States" in J.L. Esposito and I. Kalin (eds), *Islamophobia: The Challenge of Pluralism in the 21st Century* (Oxford University Press, 2011).

12 Zebiri, above.

13 S.N. Karaoglu, "A Definition of Islamophobia in Etienne Dinet's the Pilgrimage of the Sacred House of Allah" (George Washington University, 2018), see: <https://pqdtopen.proquest.com/doc/2050020599.html?FMT=ABS>.

14 E. Said, *Orientalism* (Vintage Books, 1978).

15 T. Asad, *Formations of the Secular: Christianity, Islam and Modernity* (Stanford University Press, 2003); M. Canovan, "On Economical Truths: Some Liberal Reflections", *Political Studies*, 1990, Vol. 38(1), pp. 5-19; Z. Mehdi, "Phobia of Religion: Religion as Islam a Political Argument and a Psychoanalytical Inquiry of Islamophobia in India", *International Journal of Applied Psychoanalytic Studies*, 2017, Vol. 14(3), pp. 222-244.

16 S. Lee et al., "The Islamophobia Scale", *International Journal for the Psychology of Religion*, 2009, Vol. 19(2), pp. 92-105.

17 Runnymede Trust, "Islamophobia: The Challenge For Us All" (1997), see: <http:www.runnymedetrust.org/companies/17/74/Islamophobia-A- Challenge-for- Us- All.html>.

18 T. Abbas, "After 9/11: British South Asian Muslims, Islamophobia, Multiculturalism, and the State", *American Journal of Islamic Social Sciences*, 2004, Vol. 21(3), pp. 26–38.

19 Lee, et al., "The Islamophobia Scale".

20 J. Stolz, "Explaining Islamophobia: A Test of Four Theories based on a Case of a Swiss City", *Swiss Journal of Sociology*, 2005, Vol. 31(2), pp. 547–566.

21 S. Schwartz, "The 'Islamophobes' that aren't", Frontpagemag, 28 April 2005, see: <http://www.frontpagemag/articles/read>.

22 S. Poynting and V. Mason, "The Resistible Rise of Islamophobia; Anti Muslim Racism in the UK and Australia Before 11 September 2001", 2007, *Journal of Sociology*, 2007, Vol. 43(1), pp. 61–86.

23 E. Bleich, "What Is Islamophobia and How Much Is There? Theorizing and Measuring an Emerging Comparative Concept", *American Behavioral Scientist*, 2011, Vol. 55(12), pp. 1581–1600.

24 F. Elahi and O. Khan (eds), "Islamophobia Still a Challenge For Us All" (2017), see: <https://www.runnymedetrust.org/uploads/Islamophobia%20Report%20 2018%20FINAL.pdf>.

25 K. Dunn et al., "Contemporary Racism and Islamophobia in Australia: Racializing Religion", *Ethnicities*, 2007, Vol. 7(4), pp. 564–589.

26 K.A. Beydoun, "Rethinking Islamophobia", Al Jazeera, 12 March 2018, see: <https://www.aljazeera.com/indepth/opinion/rethinking-islamophobia-180312085500278.html>.

27 T. Green, "What is Islamophobia?" in T. Green (ed.), *The Fear of Islam: An*

Introduction to Islamophobia in the West (Augsburg Publishers, 2015).

28 *Ibid.*

29 F. Halliday, "Islamophobia Reconsidered", *Ethnic and Racial Studies,* 1999, Vol. 22(5), pp. 892-902.

30 EUMC. European Monitoring Centre on Racism and Xenophobia, 2006, see <http//fra.europe.eu/en/publication/2006/highlights-eumc-report-muslims-european-union-discrimination-and -islamophibia>.

31 S. Lee et al., "The Islamophobia Scale", *International Journal for the Psychology of Religion,* 2009, Vol. 19(2), pp. 92-105.

32 Council on American–Islamic Relations (2006); *The Pew Forum on Religion and Public Life* (2007), as cited in Lee et al., above.

33 G. Bouma, "Islamophobia As a Constraint to World Peace: The Case of Australia", *Islam and Christian-Muslim Relations,* 2011 Vol. 22(4), pp. 433–441.

34 S. Akbarzadeh, "The Muslim Question in Australia: Islamophobia and Muslim Alienation", *Journal of Muslim Minority Affairs,* 2016, Vol. 36(3), pp. 323-333.

35 G. Bouma, "Islamophobia As a Constraint to World Peace: The Case of Australia", *Islam and Christian-Muslim Relations,* 2011, Vol. 22(4), pp. 433 – 441.

36 Akbarzadeh, above.

37 I. McAllister and R. Moore, "The Developments of Ethnic Prejudice: An Analysis of Australian Immigrants", *Ethnic and Racial Studies,* 1991, Vol. 14(2), pp. 127-151.

38 C. Miller, "Australia's Anti Islam Right in Their Own Words: Text as Data Analysis of Social Media Content", *Australian Journal of Political Science,* 2017, Vol. 52(3), pp. 383-401.

39 K. Dunn et al., above.

40 Bouma, above.

41 H. Auston, "New National Snapshot Finds 60 Percent Australians Would Be Concerned if a Relative Married a Muslim", *Sydney Morning Herald,* 27 September 2016.

42 L. Briskman, "The Creeping Blight of Islamophobia in Australia", *International Journal for Crime, Justice and Social Democracy,* 2015, Vol. 4(3), pp. 112-121.

43 A. Booth, A. Leigh, and E. Varganova, "Does Ethnic Discrimination Vary Across Minority Groups? Evidence From A Field Experiment", *Oxford Bulletin of Economics and Statistics,* 2012, Vol. 74(4), pp. 547-573.

44 J. Kearney and M. Taha (2015), see: <https://www.abc.net.au/news/2015-11-30/muslims-discrimination-three-times-more-than-other-australians/6985138?utm_source=abc_news&utm_medium=content_shared&utm_content=mail&utm_campaign=abc_news>.

45 D. Iner and K. Nebhan, "Islamophobia from within: A Case Study of Australian

Women" in E. Bayrakli and F. Hafiz (eds), *Islamophobia in Mulsim Majority Socities* (Routledge, 2108).

46 A. Markus, "2016 Mapping Social Cohesion Report" (2016), see: <http://Scanlonfoundation.org.au/research/surveys>.

47 *Ibid.*

48 A. Markus, "Maping Social Report Cohesion Report" (2017), see: <http://Scanlonfoundation.org.au/research/surveys>.

49 R.Hassan et al., *Australian Muslims: The Challange of Islamophobia and Social Distance* (International Center for Muslim and non-Muslim Understanding, University of South Australia, 2018).

50 L. Briskman, "The Creeping Blight of Islamophobia in Australia", *International Journal for Crime, Justice and Social Democracy,* 2015, Vol. 4(3), pp. 112-121.

51 S. Pontying and V. Mason, "The Resistible Rise of Islamophobia; Anti Muslim Racism in the UK and Australia Before 11 September 2001", *Journal of Sociology,* 2007, Vol. 43(1), pp. 61–86.

52 J.R. Goody (ed.), *Literacy in Traditional Societies* (Cambridge University Press, 1968).

53 J. Tamney, "Modernization and relgious purification: Islam in Indonesia", *Review of Religious Research,* 1980, Vol. 22(2).

54 "The Future of World Religions: Population Growth Projections 2010-2050" (Pew Research Centre, Washington DC, 2015), see: <https://www.pewforum.org/2015/04/02/religious-projections-2010-2050>.

55 R. Hassan, *Inside Muslim Minds* (Melbourne University Press, 2008); P. Werbner and T. Madood (eds), Debating Cultural Hybridity (Zed Books, 2015); C. Geertz, *Islam Observed: Religious Development in Morocco and Indonesia* (University of Chicago Press, 1968); M. Arkoun, *Rethinking Islam* (Westview Press, 1994).

56 Pew Research Center, above.

57 R. Hassan. et al., "Minority Size and Socio-Economic Inequalities: A Case Study of Muslim Minority in India", *International Sociology,* 2018, Vol. 33(3), pp. 386–406.

58 R. Hassan. R, "Trust, Ethnicity and Religion in South and Southeast Asia", *South Asia Journal,* 8 January 2019.

8. Incomprehension of religion in Australian society

1 R. Williams, *In God They Trust?: The religious beliefs of Australia's Prime Ministers, 1901-2013* (Bible Society, 2013).

2 J.H. Brookshire, *Clement Attlee* (Manchester University Press, 1995), p. 15.

3 E.G. Ellis, "Handmaids Tale Garb Is the Viral Protest Uniform of 2019", *Wired,* 5 June 2019: see <https://www.wired.com/story/handmaids-tale-protest-garb/>.

4 A.C. Grayling, *Against All Gods: Six Polemics on Religion and an Essay on Kindness* (Oberon Books, 2007), p. 15.

5 Consensus Statement on Conscientious Objection in Healthcare, 29 August 2016: see <http://blog.practicalethics.ox.ac.uk/2016/08/consensus-statement-on-conscientious-objection-in-healthcare/>; see also reply in J. Franklin, "When the prescription is a lynching", *Quadrant Online,* 21 September 2016.

6 A recent presentation with many Australian contributors is H. Ramsay (ed.), *Truth and Faith in Ethics* (Imprint Academic, 2011).

7 S. Piggin and R.D. Linder, *The Fountain of Public Prosperity: Evangelical Christians in Australian history 1740–1914* (Monash University Publishing, 2018) and *Attending to the National Soul: Evangelical Christians in Australian history 1914-2014* (Monash University Publishing, 2020).

8 W. Hudson, *Australian Religious Thought* (Monash University Publishing, 2016); also J. Franklin, "The Sydney intellectual/religious scene, 1916-2016", *St Mark's Review,* December 2017, No. 242, pp. 20-55.

9 Australian Curriculum, F-10, History Year 8 Level Description: see <https://www.australiancurriculum.edu.au/f-10-curriculum/humanities-and-social-sciences/history/?year=12319&strand=Historical+Knowledge+and+Understanding>.

10 Australian curriculum, F-10, General capabilities: Ethical understanding: see <https://www.australiancurriculum.edu.au/f-10-curriculum/general-capabilities/ethical-understanding/>.

11 J. Finnis, *Natural Law and Natural Rights* (Clarendon, 1980), pp. 87–97.

12 J. Franklin, "Freedom from religion and freedom from irreligion", *Connor Court Quarterly*, 2014, Vol. 9, pp. 1-12: see <https://web.maths.unsw.edu.au/~jim/freedomofreligion.pdf>.

13 R. Mathews, *Of Labour and Liberty: Distributism in Victoria, 1891-1966* (Monash University Publishing, 2017).

14 J. Molony, *The Worker Question: A new historical perspective on Rerum Novarum* (Collins Dove, 1991), p. 130.

15 D. Baggett and J.L. Walls, *Good God: The theistic foundations of morality* (Oxford University Press, 2011); C.S. Evans, *God and Moral Obligation* (Oxford University Press, 2014); N. Wolterstorff, *Justice: Rights and Wrongs* (Princeton University Press, 2008).

16 R. Williams, *Post-God Nation? How religion fell off the radar in Australia—and what might be done to get it back on* (ABC Books, 2005), pp. 270-1.

17 *Little Sisters of the Poor Saints Peter and Paul Home v Pennsylvania,* 591 U.S. ___ (2020).

18 Argued in M. Iles, "Israel Folau: Voters derail the PC freight train", *The Australian,* 24 May 2019.

19 Australian Bureau of Statistics, 4102.0 - Australian Social Trends, 2008: How many children have women in Australia had?: see <https://www.abs.gov.au/AUSSTATS/abs@.nsf/Lookup/4102.0Chapter3202008>.

Conclusion: Rethinking religion in a secular world

1   J. Casanova, *Global Religious and Secular Dynamics: The Modern System of Classification* (Berkley Center for Religion, Peace and World Affairs, Georgetown University, July 2019), p. 10.

2   *Ibid.*

3   R. Williams, "Overcoming Political Tribalism" in D. Freeman (ed.), *Tribalism's Troubles: Responding to Rowan Williams* (Kapunda Press, 2020), p. 3.

4   Casanova, p. 10.

5   Williams, p. 2.

6   Casanova, p. 10.

7   Pew Research Center, *The Future of World Religions: Population Growth Projections, 2010-2050* (2015), pp. 7-8. Despite the large increase in absolute numbers for these religious groups, in most cases their share of global population is not projected to change enormously over these four decades. Christians will remain at a little over 31% of world population, Hindus at approximately 15%, and Jews and "Other Religions" 0.2% and 0.7% respectively. Falls of between one and two percentage points are projected for Buddhists and folk religions (Buddhists are the only group projected to fall in absolute numbers). The notable changes in share of global population are those projected for Muslims (up 6.5 percentage points from 23.2% in 2010 to 29.7% in 2050) and the religiously unaffiliated, down 3.2 percentage points: *Ibid.*, p. 8.

8   Between 2010 and 2050, the religiously unaffiliated in Europe will increase from just under 19% to a little over 23%. The Christian share of the population will fall from 75 to 65%, while the Muslim share will increase from 6 to 10%. Europe is the only region where a decline in total population is projected over 2010 to 2050. In North America, the unaffiliated will increase from 17 to almost 26%, with the proportion of Christians decreasing from approximately 77% to 66%, and Muslims increasing from 1 to 2.4%: These changes largely reflect significant shifts in the religious composition of the United States: Ibid., p. 245.

9   In Australia during this period, the unaffiliated will rise from 24 to 40%. The proportion of Christians will fall from 67 to 47%, with Muslims increasing from 2.4 to 4.9%: *Ibid.*, p. 234.

10 Casanova, p. 41.

11 *Ibid.*, p. 39.

12 *Ibid.*, p. 18. Survey data yields interesting findings about shifts in perceptions with secularisation about the link between religion and morality or religion and social order. See Pew Research Center, *The Global God Divide* (2020); and R.F. Inglehart, "Giving up on God: The Global Decline of Religion", *Foreign Affairs,* September-October 2020.

13 Casanova, p. 39.

14 In 2017 Deloitte Access Economics estimated that members of religious

communities in Australia contribute $481 million annually in volunteering (30.5 million hours as volunteers, valued at $339 million) and charitable donations ($142 million). The report also found that religious people—that is, those who attend religious services—"are more likely to be donors and volunteers than non-religious people": SEIROS, *Economic value of donating and volunteering behaviour associated with religiosity* (2017), pp. iii and 24-25. This report was commissioned from Deloitte Access Economics by The Study of the Economic Impact of Religion on Society (SEIROS). Disclosure: I am a member of the organising committee of SEIROS. The report only examined the volunteering and donations contributed by people "who were not religious in their youth but are now", in an attempt "to untangle religiosity from other factors which might cause donating and volunteering behaviour". It is therefore a conservative estimate—in fact, an underestimate—of the contribution made by religious communities in volunteering and donations.

15 An important example concerns the amount of latitude different legal systems accord religious schools to exercise a preference ('discriminate') in employing staff in favour of those who share the religious convictions of the school community. The implication of a narrow latitude is that you can maintain a religious school with minimal religious influence; for example, that it is sufficient to preserve the religious character of the school if it is owned by the religious community and if a small number of key staff share its faith. Religious communities usually contest this minimalist approach, among other reasons because it effectively secularises a school. For an account of three major legal approaches to staffing preferences in religious schools, and an argument in favour of a narrow latitude in these matters, see R. Mężyk, "Discrimination against Employees of Religious Schools in Australia, US and the EU—A Comparison in Light of Human Rights and Deliberative Democracy", *Australian Law Journal,* 2020, vol. 94, pp. 367-80.

16 "Conscience is a judgement of reason whereby the human person recognises the moral quality of a concrete act . . ": Catechism of the Catholic Church (1994), §. 1778. It is distinguished from relativism or mere freedom of opinion by its relationship to the truth. A traditional formulation of conscience in this regard was provided by the Second Vatican Council: "deep within his conscience man discovers a law which he has not laid upon himself but which he must obey": *Gaudium et spes,* Pastoral Constitution on the Church in the Modern World, 7 December 1965, §. 16

17 Inglehart, p. 111.

18 *Ibid.,* pp. 115-16.

19 *Ibid.,* p. 118.

Index

www.ingramcontent.com/pod-product-compliance
Lightning Source LLC
Chambersburg PA
CBHW071018280326
41935CB00011B/1407